The Thirteen Colonies

# Massachusetts

**Books in the Thirteen Colonies series include:**

## The Thirteen Colonies

# Massachusetts

Lydia Bjornlund

Lucent Books, Inc.
P.O. Box 289011, San Diego, California

*To Jake and Sophia*

Library of Congress Cataloging-in-Publication Data

Bjornlund, Lydia D.
  Massachusetts / by Lydia Bjornlund.
    p. cm. — (The thirteen colonies)
  Includes bibliographical references and index.
  ISBN 1-56006-879-5 (hardback : alk. paper)
  1. Massachusetts—History—1775–1865—Juvenile literature.
[1. Massachusetts—History—Colonial period, ca. 1600–1775. 2.
Massachusetts—History—1775–1865.] I. Title. II. Thirteen
colonies (Lucent Books)
  F67 .B66 2001
  974.4'02—dc21
                                                    2001001758

# Contents

# Foreword

The story of the thirteen English colonies that became the United States of America is one of startling diversity, conflict, and cultural evolution. Today, it is easy to assume that the colonists were of one mind when fighting for independence from England and afterwards when the national government was created. However, the American colonies had to overcome a vast reservoir of distrust rooted in the broad geographical, economic, and social differences that separated them. Even the size of the colonies contributed to the conflict; the smaller states feared domination by the larger ones.

These sectional differences stemmed from the colonies' earliest days. The northern colonies were more populous and their economies were more diverse, being based on both agriculture and manufacturing. The southern colonies, however, were dependent on agriculture—in most cases, the export of only one or two staple crops. These economic differences led to disagreements over things such as the trade embargo the Continental Congress imposed against England during the war. The southern colonies wanted their staple crops to be exempt from the embargo because their economies would have collapsed if they could not trade with England, which in some cases was the sole importer. A compromise was eventually made and the southern colonies were allowed to keep trading some exports.

In addition to clashing over economic issues, often the colonies did not see eye to eye on basic political philosophy. For example, Connecticut leaders held that education was the route to greater political liberty, believing that knowledgeable citizens would not allow themselves to be stripped of basic freedoms and rights. South Carolinians, on the other hand, thought that the protection of personal property and economic independence was the basic foundation of freedom. In light of such profound differences it is amazing that the colonies were able to unite in the fight for independence and then later under a strong national government.

Why, then, did the colonies unite? When the Revolutionary War began the colonies set aside their differences and banded together because they shared a common goal—gaining political freedom from what they considered a tyrannical monarchy—that could be more easily attained if they cooperated with each other. However, after the war ended, the states abandoned unity and once again pursued sectional interests, functioning as little nations in a weak confederacy. The congress of this confederacy, which was bound by the Articles of Confederation, had virtually no authority over the individual states. Much bickering ensued— the individual states refused to pay their war debts to the national government, the nation was sinking further into an economic depression, and there was nothing the national government could do. Political leaders realized that the nation was in jeopardy of falling apart. They were also aware that European nations such as England, France, and Spain were all watching the new country, ready to conquer it at the first opportunity. Thus the states came together at the Constitutional Convention in order to create a system of government that would be both strong enough to protect them from invasion and yet nonthreatening to state interests and individual liberties.

The Thirteen Colonies series affords the reader a thorough understanding of how the development of the individual colonies helped create the United States. The series examines the early history of each colony's geographical region, the founding and first years of each colony, daily life in the colonies, and each colony's role in the American Revolution. Emphasis is given to the political, economic, and social uniqueness of each colony. Both primary and secondary quotes enliven the text, and sidebars highlight personalities, legends, and personal stories. Each volume ends with a chapter on how the colony dealt with changes after the war and its role in developing the U.S. Constitution and the new nation. Together, the books in this series convey a remarkable story—how thirteen fiercely independent colonies came together in an unprecedented political experiment that not only succeeded, but endures to this day.

# Introduction

# The Bay State

Massachusetts, which has been nicknamed "the Bay State," is a small state with a big history. When the Pilgrims landed on a rocky peninsula they named Plimouth (now spelled *Plymouth*) in the fall of 1620, they founded the second English colony in the New World. Within just a couple of decades, thousands of their countrymen had followed, founding settlements along the coast of present-day Massachusetts. Gradually, people moved inland in search of land, clearing forests to build their houses, graze their animals, and plant their crops.

Although the rocky soil made farming difficult and the weather was cold, the settlers managed to forge a life for themselves, gradually becoming a leading force in the economy of the British colonies. The settlers were also leaders in education. Massachusetts was home to the first public school, the first college, the first public library, and the first newspaper in the colonies. The colony also became an integral part of the eventual fight against England. Samuel Adams, Paul Revere, John Hancock—all of these icons of America's fight for freedom hailed from Massachusetts. Massachusetts was the site of the Revolutionary War's first battles—and one of its bloodiest.

The founders of the colony of Massachusetts brought with them their English customs and heritage. Over time, they adapted these to meet their new needs and circumstances and learned new ways of doing things from their Native American neighbors. Historian Benjamin W. Labaree explains in his book on colonial Massachusetts:

Samuel Adams, a Massachusetts leader in the colonies' struggle for independence from England.

Before the close of the century . . . most of the Old World values brought by the immigrant generation were altered beyond recognition. . . . The habit of looking to the mother country in cultural matters continued but was challenged by an awakening self-awareness by the colonists. [1]

By the end of the colonial era, the people of Massachusetts were different from any others—their English roots and new circumstances had forged a unique character. They were no longer English, they were "Yankee."

## Chapter One

# In the Beginning

Long before the first permanent settlement was founded at Plymouth, European explorers and fishermen wrote home of the bounty that could be found in the area in and around present-day Massachusetts. Europeans made several attempts to settle in this new land, but the first men who tried it were not prepared for the harsh winters and difficult conditions so far from home. News of rich, uninhabited lands would reach England, however, enticing a new wave of settlers across the Atlantic.

In reality, New England was neither rich nor uninhabited. Thousands of people lived on the land. The coming of the Europeans would change forever the lives of these Native American peoples.

### Before the Europeans

When Europeans first reached the land that is currently Massachusetts, several small tribes inhabited the area. The Pocomtuc lived in the western part of the state, the Nipmuc in central Massachusetts, the Pennacook in northern Massachusetts and parts of New Hampshire and Vermont, the Massachuset in the Boston area, the Wampanoag in southern Massachusetts, and the Nauset in Cape Cod and the islands off Massachusetts. Each of these tribes occupied a different region and operated independently of the others, but they shared a common heritage as part of the Algonquian family.

Like other Native Americans, the Algonquian began as hunters and gatherers. Over time, they began to cultivate crops. By the seventeenth century, they had settled in villages, some of which were home to as many as four hundred people. Villages were maintained as long as the land could support the farming and the nearby woods the hunting. Every ten years or so, the village would move, and the old site would revert to forest.

## The Algonquian Lifestyle

The Algonquian lived in dome-shaped huts called wigwams. Wigwams were made of wooden poles that were bent and covered with tree bark. Each wigwam was the home of several families, related through the female line. One early observer described the wigwam as "very strong and handsome, covered with close wrought mats, made by their women of flagges, rushes, and hempen threds, so defensive, that neither raine . . . nor winde can enter." [2] At the center of the wigwam was a fire pit used for cooking and to warm the dwelling.

The women of the village were responsible for growing the crops, which consisted primarily of corn, beans, squash, and pumpkins. To supplement this diet, women gathered berries, nuts, and maple sap

Algonquian tribes lived in wigwams which sometimes housed several families.

from the nearby forests. Men hunted deer, bears, rabbits, otter, beaver, and wild turkeys and caught fish in the many rivers and lakes. Migrating ducks, geese, and passenger pigeons were shot with bows and arrows. In addition, tribes that lived along the shore used nets to catch the large fish in the Atlantic Ocean and gathered shellfish from the ocean floor.

The several tribes that shared the region of New England made both war and peace with one another. Over the centuries, they had forged a life amid the wilderness. Historian Richard D. Brown explains, "When the English arrived at the beginning of the seventeenth century, they found a comparatively old and stable system of rivalries among the tribes and their neighbors."[3]

The Indians had coexisted for many years, but contact with European explorers, fishermen, and fur traders changed their lives forever. Like other Native Americans, the tribes of Massachusetts were hit hard by smallpox, measles, and other diseases because, unlike Europeans, they had no immunity to such diseases. By 1620, the Indian population in Massachusetts had been reduced by almost two-thirds, and entire villages had been wiped out. The English settlers took this as a sign from God that the land was theirs for the taking.

## Exploration and Discovery

Historians believe that the first Europeans to visit North America were the Vikings. Their trip to Newfoundland is well documented, and some believe their travels took them as far south as Massachusetts. The next Europeans to set foot in present-day New England, however, came several centuries later. Miguel Côrte-Real, a Portuguese explorer, lived among the Indians of New England after he was shipwrecked off the coast in 1502. In 1524, Giovanni da Verrazano, an Italian explorer employed by France, visited the shores of Massachusetts as he explored the Atlantic Coast between the New York and Narragansett Bays. The next year, Esteban Gómez, a Portuguese captain sailing for Spain, charted the coast between Massachusetts Bay and Cape Cod.

Many explorers for Italy, France, Spain, Portugal, and England followed suit in the century to come, sailing across the Atlantic Ocean to what they called the "New World." Some came in search of a passage to the Pacific Ocean, but others planned to stay. European countries sponsored expeditions in search of gold and other riches, fertile land on which to settle, and friendly Native Americans with whom to trade.

## News of the New World

In 1602, English explorer Bartholomew Gosnold commanded the *Concord* as it sailed along the North American coast from Maine to Rhode Island. According to historian

In 1524, Giovanni da Verrazano explored the coast of Massachusetts along with other areas of the Atlantic coastline.

Douglas Edward Leach, "Gosnold had come with a purpose: to plant a small settlement to serve primarily as a base for economic exploitation of the country."[4] Along his way, Gosnold named Cape Cod, some of the islands in Nantucket Sound, including Martha's Vineyard, and the Elizabeth Islands. On one of these islands, now called Cuttyhunk, Gosnold and his twenty men built a house and a fort. They planned to establish a permanent settlement, but they soon realized that their meager supplies would last only about six weeks, and headed home for England.

When they got home, Bartholomew Gosnold and his men spoke about what they had found on their voyage. They raved about the fishing near Cape Cod and the sparsely populated land that stretched as far as the eye could see. One crewman reported that it was "the goodliest continent that ever we saw, promising more by farre than we any way did expect."[5]

By this time, European fishermen were familiar with the northern Atlantic, lured by the excellent fishing conditions. Even in winter, the catch was good. Lobster and shellfish were so plentiful along the Massachusetts coast that the Indians used them for bait or to feed their livestock, and the Europeans soon followed their example. Some fishermen set up camps in Newfoundland and Nova Scotia, where they spent their summers drying the fish they caught before returning across the Atlantic to sell it at market. The camps served as a base of operations from which explorers mapped territories to the south, including Massachusetts.

In 1605, Sir George Weymouth, an Englishman, visited the coasts of Nantucket and Maine. Like Gosnold, he was highly optimistic about the area's possibilities for trade and settlement. An added impetus to England's interest in the New World was competition from France. England feared that its longtime rival might get the upper hand, economically or militarily, from its foothold in the Americas. In 1605 and 1606, French explorer Samuel de Champlain carefully charted parts of the Massachusetts coast in search of a suitable site for a settlement, but France instead chose to build its settlements farther north.

## The First Settlements

In 1607, England sent another expedition with 120 men to establish a trading settlement. This time a colony was attempted at Sagadahoc at the mouth of the Kennebec River in present-day Maine. The settlers built a fort, a church, a storehouse, and fifteen homes. After only one winter, they abandoned their effort and fled for England aboard the ship that had come to bring them additional supplies.

England was keen on establishing more permanent roots in the New World, however. One historian explains:

> Peace with Spain was in the offing, and new possibilities for trade were in prospect. Even the most northern parts of America now appeared attractive, since it was now appreciated that the seas there abounded with fish, while the land contained many fur-bearing animals. [6]

When the London Company, a group of English merchants seeking profit, set their sights on the New World, they hired John Smith to lead the expedition. In 1607, Smith and his men set up camp at the mouth of a small river. Jamestown, Virginia, would become the first permanent English settlement.

Smith became a leader of Jamestown, and his astute leadership was responsible for much of the colony's early survival and success. A serious injury forced him to return from Jamestown to England, but he longed to revisit the world he had pioneered. He jumped at the chance to join a fur-trading expedition to an area far north of Virginia in 1614. He called the region he visited New England and named one area Massachusetts after the Indians who lived there. Massachusetts is believed to mean "the place of the great hill."

## A Difficult Life in England

In 1616, Smith published *A Description of New England*. This description caught the attention of many people in England. The thought of starting over in the new world Smith and others described intrigued them because their lives were becoming more and more difficult. First, changes to the English economy were displacing many people from the farms on which they had lived for generations. The price of wool was going up, causing many landlords to switch from farming to sheep ranching. Since farming was no longer an option for the peasants who lived on this land, many moved to cities in search of other work. The population of England's cities swelled with unemployed, unskilled laborers. Those who could find work were paid a meager wage. Even skilled artisans could barely earn enough money to survive.

The country was also in political and religious turmoil. By law, people in England had to support the Church of England (also known as the Anglican Church). Practicing a different religion was illegal, subject to imprisonment and even death. Despite these laws, many people did not like the Church of England. Among these were people who wanted to reform—or "purify"—the religion by making the services simpler and focusing more attention

John Smith published *A Description of New England* in 1616.

on the Bible. They became known as Puritans. Another group believed that the church was too corrupt to be reformed and wanted to leave the Church of England entirely to set up a more godly church of their own. They became known as Separatists.

## The Separatists Search for a New Life

The Separatists longed for a place to practice their religion freely. In 1608 William Brewster led a group of Separatists from Scrooby, England, to settle in Leyden, a small town in the Netherlands. They were uneasy in their new environment, however. They worried that the liberal lifestyle of the Dutch would have a bad influence on their children. In addition, most of the jobs they could find in Holland paid little. When news of the "New World" across the Atlantic reached the town of Leyden, some of the Separatists living there saw this as an opportunity to start a community that would be insulated from outside influences. It sounded like a dream come true. Perhaps on the other side of the ocean they would be able to live according to God's word.

In 1620, a small group of people set out from England on two leaky ships across the Atlantic Ocean. Their trip was hazardous; in fact they had to return just days after setting sail because one of the ships—the *Speedwell*—was taking on water. Some of the *Speedwell*'s passengers

In 1620, the *Mayflower* carried 101 Pilgrims from England to the New World.

# Mayflower Compact

*In 1620, thirty-five Separatist men, women, and children set out across the Atlantic Ocean. Also on board were about sixty-six "strangers"—non-Separatist artisans, soldiers, and indentured servants who sought a new life in the New World. As they prepared to land at Plymouth in Massachusetts Bay, some of the passengers declared that the contract that was to rule them in Virginia had no authority. Recognizing that survival depended on orderly behavior as a community, the Pilgrim leaders asked the men to join in a covenant, much like the covenant that governed their church. Anchored offshore, they signed what came to be known as the* Mayflower Compact. *The following is reprinted from* "The American Revolution: An HTML Project" *(http://odur.let.rug.nl/~usa/D/1601-1650/plymouth/compac.htm).*

In The Name of God, Amen. We, whose names are underwritten, the Loyal Subjects of our dread Sovereign Lord King James, by the Grace of God, of Great Britain, France, and Ireland, King, Defender of the Faith, &c. Having undertaken for the Glory of God, and Advancement of the Christian Faith, and the Honor of our King and Country, a Voyage to plant the first colony in the northern Parts of Virginia; Do by these Presents, solemnly and mutually in the Presence of God and one another, covenant and combine ourselves together into a civil Body Politick, for our better Ordering and Preservation, and Furtherance of the Ends aforesaid; And by Virtue hereof do enact, constitute, and frame, such just and equal Laws, Ordinances, Acts, Constitutions, and Offices, from time to time, as shall be thought most meet and convenient for the general Good of the Colony; unto which we promise all due Submission and Obedience. In WITNESS whereof we have hereunto subscribed our names at Cape Cod the eleventh of November, in the Reign of our Sovereign Lord King James of England, France, and Ireland, the eighteenth and of Scotland, the fifty-fourth. Anno Domini, 1620.

joined the group on the *Mayflower;* others remained in England hoping for another chance to make their way to the New World.

In all, there were 101 passengers on the *Mayflower.* Not all of them were Separatists, however. Also on board were non-Puritan artisans, soldiers, indentured servants, and others who had both a desire to leave England and skills that the Separatists believed might be needed. The Puritans called them "strangers."

When they set sail across the Atlantic, the passengers—Separatists and strangers alike—became known as the Pilgrims.

## The Mayflower Compact

The Pilgrims had set sail for Virginia, but winds blew them far to the north of their intended landing spot. They dropped anchor in a sheltered harbor off the tip of Cape Cod and decided to forge a settlement on a promising parcel of land on the coast. They called the area Plymouth, after their point of departure in England.

With this turn of events, some of the passengers declared that the contract that was to rule them in Virginia had no authority in this strange land. William Bradford, a leader of the Pilgrims, later recalled that the passengers threatened that when they "came ashore they would use their own liberty, for none had power to command them."[7]

Bradford and his colleagues were alarmed by this turn of events. They knew that survival depended on orderly behavior as a community. Bradford proposed that they join in a covenant, much like the covenant that governed their church. Anchored offshore, the Pilgrims signed what has come to be known as the Mayflower Compact. The signers agreed to "covenant and combine ourselves together into a civil Body Politick, for our better Ordering and Preservation" and to make and abide by "Laws, Ordinances, Acts, Constitutions, and Officers, from time to time, as shall be thought most meet and convenient for the general Good of the Colony."[8]

In effect, the Mayflower Compact established a government based on the consent of the governed. The people themselves agreed to live by the laws that were made. As other communities in the New World followed in the footsteps of the Pilgrims, the Mayflower Compact set a precedent for self-government. Historian Douglas Edward Leach writes:

> [The Mayflower Compact was] the first example of what has become known as a "plantation covenant" . . . that is, a written compact among a group of pioneers who, finding themselves

# A View from William Bradford

*In their quest for a better community, the Pilgrims faced the unknown head-on, putting their faith in God to see to their safety. William Bradford was among the leaders during the voyage and served as one of the first governors of Plymouth Plantation. In this excerpt from* Of Plimouth Plantation, *Bradford describes what it was like to be a Pilgrim getting ready to disembark from the Mayflower.*

Here I cannot but pause and stand amazed, and so, too, I think will the reader when he considers this poor people and their present condition. For they had no dwelling places for their weatherbeaten bodies; no houses or much less towns to repair to, to seek for succor. And for the season it was winter, and they that know the winters of that country [New England] know them to be sharp and violent, and subject to cruel and fierce storms, dangerous to travel to known places, much more to search an unknown coast. Besides what could they see but a hideous and desolate wilderness, full of wild beasts and wild men—and what multitudes there might be of them they knew not. Nor could they ... view ... a more goodly country to feed their hopes; for which way soever they turned their eyes (save upward to the heavens) they would have little solace or content in respect of any outward objects. For summer being done, all things stand upon them with a weatherbeaten face, and the whole country, full of woods and thickets represented a wild and savage hue. . . . If they looked behind them, there was the mighty ocean over which they had passed and was now a main bar and gulf to separate them from all the civil parts of the world. . . . What could now sustain them but the spirit of God and His Grace?

William Bradford, a Pilgrim and one of the first governors of Plymouth Plantation.

outside the protecting arm of the law, establish a basis for law among themselves. . . . The Pilgrims . . . simply faced up to potential anarchy [lawlessness] and, drawing upon experience and common sense fortified with a firm determination to make things work out right, devised a practical way to prevent it.[9]

The document marked the beginning of a new feeling in colonial America—a feeling that the colonists were separate from their mother country.

## Chapter Two

# The First Settlers

Life for the Pilgrims was not easy. Most were from the cities and towns of England and had little or no experience in forging a community out of the wilderness. Only a few were familiar with farming—a skill that would be necessary to their very survival. Yet from these humble beginnings, the Pilgrims not only survived but thrived. Soon, following in their footsteps came others who were hungry for a new beginning, and the colony began to grow in size and stature.

On November 21, 1620, after a treacherous journey that had taken over two months, the Pilgrims prepared to go ashore. Wrote Bradford, "Being thus arrived in a good harbor and brought safe to land, they [the Pilgrims] fell upon their knees and blessed the God of heaven who had brought them over the vast and furious ocean, and deliverd them from all the perils and miseries thereof."[10]

The Pilgrims were pleased with their new home. The dense woods were a rich source of food and provided an abundance of wood to build homes and fires. Fowl inhabited the marshes, and fish abounded in the sea.

Life in the new land was difficult, however. The Pilgrims had anticipated having other English colonists to help them get settled. Now, they had to rely solely on themselves, foraging as best they could for food to supplement the meager provisions they brought with them on the *Mayflower*. The colonists had also planned to establish their village in the warmer climate of Virginia. In Massachusetts, the ground was frozen, and it was too late in the season to plant crops.

The Pilgrims first landed at Plymouth, December, 1620.

Furthermore, poor nutrition and a lack of fresh air on the voyage had left the settlers weak. Many suffered from scurvy—a disease caused by a lack of vitamin C—or other dietary deficiencies. During that first winter, nearly half of the colonists died, including all but four of the women.

## Native American Friends and Allies

The settlement may not have survived had the Pilgrims not had good neighbors. One day in the early spring of 1621, an Indian named Samoset strode into Plymouth and introduced himself in broken English. A short time later, he returned with Squanto, who spoke very good English because he had been kidnapped by English explorers. Squanto stayed with the Pilgrims and taught them some of the Indian ways. He showed them the best fishing spots and how to dig for clams at low tide. He explained which plants grew well in the Massachusetts climate and how to plant them in the rocky soil. He also taught them to use fish for fertilizer and to cut around the trees so that the crops were in direct sunlight. William Bradford called Squanto "a special instrument sent of God."[11]

Squanto also introduced the English settlers to Massasoit, a powerful Wampanoag chief. Massasoit and the leaders of Plymouth Plantation made a peace treaty, declaring that neither would harm the other and that they would aid one another if attacked. The peace

# Squanto

Not many details are known about Squanto, but the legend of his life among the Pilgrims lives on. A member of the Pawtuxet band of the Wampanoag tribe, Squanto was one of twenty Pawtuxet Indians kidnapped by English explorer Thomas Hunt and sold into slavery in Spain. Squanto made his way to England, where he learned English. Thomas Dermer, another English explorer, enlisted him as a guide and interpreter on his voyages to Newfoundland in 1617 and to present-day Massachusetts in 1619. Squanto remained loyal to Dermer until Dermer was killed in a skirmish with the Spanish in 1620.

When Squanto returned to the land of his birth, he found his village abandoned and learned that an epidemic had wiped out the Pawtuxet people. Squanto was living among the Wampanoag, perhaps as their captive, when he was sent to live with the English settlers.

Squanto taught the English how to plant Indian corn and other vegetables and to use fish as fertilizer. He also introduced the colonists to neighboring tribes, enabling them to establish vital trade relationships early on. He also was instrumental in forging a relationship between the Pilgrims and Massasoit, the leader of the neighboring Wampanoag. The peace would last until Massasoit's death many decades later.

Some historians have written that without the help of Squanto, the Pilgrims would not have survived their first winter. Others believe that Squanto's role in the history of Plymouth Plantation has been overstated. Regardless, there is little doubt that the Pilgrims themselves were grateful for his help. William Bradford, an early leader of Plymouth Plantation, wrote that Squanto was an "instrument sent of God."

Squanto taught the Pilgrims how to plant corn and other vegetables.

was critical to the survival of the little colony during its fledgling years. One resident of Plymouth called Indians "the most cruellest and trecherousest people in all these parts, even like Lyons, but to us they have beene like Lambes, so kinde, so submissive, and trustie, as a man may truly say many Christians are not so kinde, nor sincere."[12]

By the next fall, the Pilgrims had, in Bradford's words, "all things in good plenty." Bradford organized a feast of thanksgiving and invited Massasoit to celebrate their first harvest. Massasoit arrived with about

# Massachusetts Bay's Charter

*The formation of the Massachusetts Bay Colony differed from that of Plymouth. First and foremost, it was a business proposition, in which investors assumed that the New World would reap great rewards. The following description of the Massachusetts Bay Colony's 1629 charter was written by Danny Barnhoorn for "The American Revolution: An HTML Project," (http://odur.let.rug.nl/~usa/D/1601–1650/massachusetts/mchart_i.htm).*

The charter of Massachusetts Bay represents still another way in which self-government was established in the English colonies of North America. In this case, the Massachusetts Bay Company, a joint-stock company resident in England, whose membership included merchants and landed gentry, received a charter from the Crown. The government of the company and the extent of its authority were clearly stated in the charter, with an unstated premise that the management of the company and thus the charter itself would remain in England.

However, a group of Puritans within the Massachusetts Bay Company adopted a pledge known as the Cambridge Agreement, in which they stipulated that they would not only migrate to the New World but also carry the charter with them. This last step was taken to assure those Puritans in the company who settled in New England that they would retain control of company management. By bringing the charter to America, the Puritans took the first step in transforming Massachusetts Bay from a trading company into a commonwealth, because the charter became the constitution of the colony.

ninety men from his tribe; Bradford wrote that "for three days we entertained [them] and feasted." [13]

## "A City upon a Hill"

Soon after that early celebration, another ship arrived bringing settlers. The new immigrants joined the Pilgrims or settled in small fishing villages to the north of Plymouth. Historian Douglas Edward Leach writes, "Plymouth watched the appearance of these pioneering communities . . . with a combination of relief and apprehension— relief because they meant added strength against the forces of the wilderness, apprehension because they brought with them to America the worldly corruption that the Pilgrims were trying to escape." [14]

The most influential of these immigrants were the Puritans, who settled along the shore of Massachusetts Bay beginning in 1630. The Puritans brought a charter from England's king, granting them title to the land and setting rules about how the colony would be run. Under the leadership of John Winthrop, they set out to build a godly place that would set an example for the world to follow. Winthrop described their goals:

> To do justly, to love mercy, to walk humbly with our God. For this end we must be knit together in this work as one man; we must entertain each other in brotherly affection; we must be willing to abridge ourselves of our superflities for the supply of others' necessities . . . rejoice together, mourn together, labor and suffer together always having before our eyes our commission and community in the work. . . . For we must consider that we shall be as a city upon a hill, the eyes of all people are upon us. [15]

The Puritans were better equipped, better financed, and better organized than the Pilgrims. On the whole, they were well educated and prosperous; according to writer Edwin Tunis, they were "socially, economically, and intellectually a cut above the Plymouth settlers." [16] They set about establishing a community of which they could be proud.

Trade of goods with the Indians greatly contributed to the survival of the English colonists.

From the beginning, the Massachusetts Bay Colony dwarfed Plymouth. By the end of the summer, more than one thousand settlers were living in small, scattered communities along the bay. By the end of 1630, eleven towns had been established. This number would grow: by 1647, there were thirty-three towns in Massachusetts. The largest of these was Boston, which was founded by Winthrop and his Puritan followers in 1630 and made the capital of the Massachusetts Bay Colony in 1632.

## Trade with the Indians

The English colonists living in Plymouth, Boston, and the small villages along the coast were not the only inhabitants of Massachusetts, however. There remained tens of thousands of Indians—indeed, until the late 1600s there were more Indians than

English in New England. Many, like Massasoit, chose to forge alliances with their new neighbors. They saw their new neighbors as a steady source of guns and other sophisticated weapons that became increasingly necessary to fight off their enemies.

In fact, it was the Indian trade that enabled the early English settlers to survive. Fishing and farming were inadequate, as historian Richard Middleton explains:

> The initial expectation was that fishing and fur trading would be sufficiently profitable to fulfill their agreement with the merchants [who had sponsored their trip]. Some attempts were made to build fishing vessels, but most Pilgrims devoted themselves to farming, since this is what they were accustomed to do. Unfortunately, farming in the area offered subsistence at best, even when carried out communally. [17]

Like the Indians, the English colonists became increasingly dependent on trade for their livelihood. In return for axes, metal goods, guns, and ammunition, they received furs from beavers and other animals, which were used to make hats that were in vogue in Europe at the time. "The Pilgrims quickly demonstrated both imagination and adaptability, qualities much to be prized on a wilderness frontier," writes Douglas

## Population of Massachusetts

| | | |
|---|---|---|
| 1620 | 102 | |
| 1630 | 2,000 | |
| 1645 | 18,000 | |
| 1670 | 60,000 | |
| 1700 | 80,000 | |
| 1725 | 110,000 | |
| 1750 | 122,000 | Dale Taylor, *A Writers Guide to Everyday Life in Colonial America.* |
| 1776 | 338,667 | |

Edward Leach. "Business flourished, and year after year large quantities of skins and furs, especially beaver, were shipped to England to help pay the colony's debts."[18]

The trade alliances between the European settlers and their native neighbors would change forever the destiny of the Indians. Before European contact, New England's Indians used tools made from wood, stone, and shells. Soon after they met Europeans, however, they almost immediately became dependent on them for metal axes, hoes, knives, and firearms and ammunition. One expert explains in *Through Indian Eyes:*

> As the people grew accustomed to metal tools, they lost the arts of chipping flint into arrowheads and shaping pieces of bone into knives and scrapers. As a result, foreign-made articles that began as luxuries were soon necessities. Without metal farm tools, Indian villagers could not raise enough food to sustain themselves. They were growing dependent on the white traders for their very survival.[19]

Competition for good hunting grounds made the rivalry among tribes more combative, and the firearms they obtained from Europeans made combat more deadly. Within a few decades, many Indian villages—and even entire tribes—would be wiped out.

## War and Peace Among the Indians

The peace treaty that the Pilgrims had made with Massasoit lasted over forty years. During this time, new English towns sprang up in areas once occupied by Native Americans. As wave after wave of immigrants crossed the Atlantic, they established new settlements farther and farther from the populated coast. Other colonists moved inland in search of better soil and to be closer to fertile hunting grounds and the fur trade. By the time Massasoit died in 1660, the Massachusetts Bay Colony had more than one hundred thousand people in towns as far west as Northampton, and the population in Plymouth numbered an additional ten thousand.

An increasing number of Native Americans were becoming angry about the English colonists' continual encroachment on their lands.

After becoming chief of the Wampanoag in 1661, Metacomet led a crusade to prevent colonists from claiming more land.

When Massasoit's son Metacomet—known as "King Philip" to the English—became chief in 1661, he began to try to regain some of the Wampanoags' land. He forged alliances with other Native American groups living in New England to put a stop to the spread of colonial villages.

In 1675, a white settler shot and injured a Wampanoag Indian near Swansea, a town in the southern part of Plymouth Colony. Metacomet and a group of Wampanoag warriors retaliated, burning Swansea and killing several of the colonists who lived there. This was the beginning of a series of raids and counterraids that became known as King Philip's War. Over the next several months, Wampanoag, Narragansett, Abenaki, Nipmuc, and Mohawk tribes battled colonial militia from towns throughout New England. Outnumbered and outgunned, the Native Americans were weaker with each battle. When

Metacomet was killed in August 1676, his colleagues in arms surrendered.

More than one thousand colonists and even more Indians lost their lives in the fight. Thirteen English settlements were completely destroyed; several others were partially damaged. "Whatever hope there may have been in 1675 of a racial accommodation," writes

The series of raids and counterraids that became known as King Philip's War put a halt to the fragile peace between Native Americans and English settlers.

historian Benjamin Labaree, "disappeared in the smoke of King Philip's War." [20]

King Philip's War left the colonies in Massachusetts stronger than ever. Massachusetts Bay had come to the aid of its smaller neighbor Plymouth, strengthening the bond among the two colonies. In addition, many of the Native Americans who had been involved in the war left their native lands for Canada, leaving behind fertile lands that were quickly swept up by the waves of immigrants coming from England and other parts of Europe.

## Seeds of Malcontent

As the threat from the Native Americans subsided, another threat—that of the mother country—began to loom large, as laws passed in England threatened the economy of Massachusetts and the livelihood of those who lived there.

By the late 1600s, Massachusetts had begun to produce and export a variety of valuable goods. The Massachusetts colonists engaged in profitable trade with a number of partners in addition to England and other British colonies—the West Indies, Holland, France, and Spain. England was threatened by its rivals and decided on a policy to restrict the rights of colonists to trade freely. Laws were enacted that required the colonists to conduct most of their trade with England and to use only ships that were manufactured, owned, and captained by people in England or the English colonies.

These so-called Navigation Acts initiated a series of events that would culminate in the American Revolution. Historian Samuel Eliot Morison writes, "Boston became the headquarters of the American Revolution largely because the policy of George III [the king of England] threatened her maritime interests." [21]

Colonists in Boston and other ports along the Massachusetts coast refused to comply with the legislation. After all, they had struggled to carve a living out of the untamed land with little help from England. Why should England profit from their labors? Colonial merchants could make more money trading elsewhere, so why should they be forced to trade with the English? The merchants of Massachusetts simply ignored the Navigation Acts and resorted to smuggling to trade the items they wanted.

Sir Edmund Andros, in 1684, was chosen to govern a cluster of states called the Dominion of New England.

## England Clamps Down

England could do little to stop the smuggling on the high seas, which continued for several decades. Upon taking the throne, however, King Charles II was determined to put a stop to Massachusetts's defiance and to tighten his control over the colony. In 1684, he revoked Massachusetts Bay's charter and made it a royal colony under his direct control. Shortly thereafter, Massachusetts Bay Colony, Plymouth Colony, New Hampshire, Rhode Island, Connecticut, New Jersey, and New York were combined into a single province called the Dominion of New England. Sir Edmund Andros was chosen to govern this new colony.

Andros believed the best way to deal with the colonists was to take decisive action and strict control. He forbade town meetings and denied the colonists a voice in the government. He imposed several new taxes and required people to pay rent on the land. Those who opposed him were jailed and fined. The colonists hated him, and when King James II, brother of Charles II, was overthrown by Protestants in England just two and a half years later, the colonists took advantage of the turmoil to capture Andros and reestablish self-rule.

The new king and queen, William and Mary, feared giving the high-spirited colonists too much control, but they also recognized that tightening controls would only further antagonize them. They compromised by merging Massachusetts Bay and Plymouth into one colony and declaring that although it would be a royal colony, the colonists would be allowed to run many of their own affairs through an elected colonial legislature. The place would be known as Massachusetts.

## The Seeds of Independence

The new charter that went into effect in 1691 was unique among the colonies. In other royal colonies, the king selected the governor and his council. In Massachusetts, the king selected the governor, but the governor's council was elected annually by the General Court, whose members were in turn elected by the colonists. This gave the people significant political power over colonial affairs.

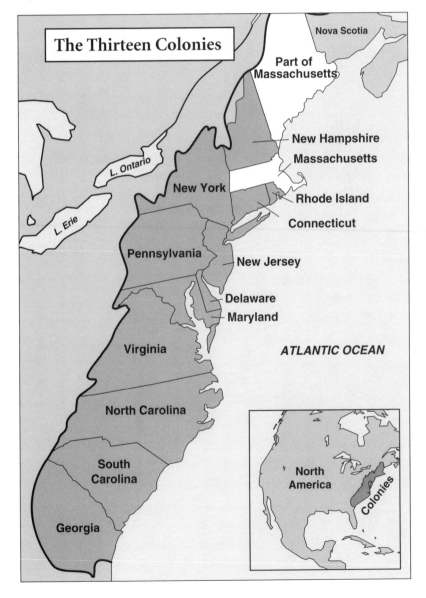

The Thirteen Colonies

Nova Scotia

Part of Massachusetts

L. Ontario

New Hampshire

Massachusetts

New York

Rhode Island

L. Erie

Connecticut

Pennsylvania

New Jersey

Delaware

Maryland

Virginia

ATLANTIC OCEAN

North Carolina

South Carolina

North America

Colonies

Georgia

The colonists had also won an important philosophical battle. They had opposed the king and won. No longer did they see themselves as mere subjects of England at the mercy of the whims of the king or Parliament. In fact, an increasing number felt little loyalty toward England, and hardly considered themselves English at all. They had a new identity—as Americans.

## Chapter Three

# Life in Colonial Massachusetts

From the time the first settlers set foot in Massachusetts, others followed. The population growth was immediate and steady. By 1640 Plymouth Colony had added seven new towns, and Massachusetts Bay had about fifteen. By 1690, Boston had a population of seven thousand—a number that more than doubled in the next fifty years. For most of the colonial period, Boston remained the largest town in the colonies.

In their quest for land, settlers had begun to push outward from the coast. Of the eighty-three towns that existed in 1695, twenty were farther than a day's travel from Boston. By 1713, the first settlements were founded in the western part of the state, at Sheffield and Stockbridge.

By this time, many other American colonies numbered among their peoples a substantial number of immigrants from Ireland, Scotland, Germany, and other parts of Europe, as well as a few thousand African slaves. The American colonists often welcomed these newcomers, who bolstered their numbers and served as a buffer between them and French, Spanish, and Indian settlements. However, most Massachusetts settlers were against the idea of settlement by anyone other than fellow Englishmen, and argued that only poverty and slovenliness would come from allowing foreigners to settle in

The first settlers in Massachusetts quickly developed their own, uniquely American, way of life.

their midst. As a result, Massachusetts remained of mostly English stock—what one historian calls "strikingly homogeneous."[22]

In many ways, however, Massachusetts had grown beyond its English roots. The colonists who lived there no longer abided by the purely English way of doing things. Instead, they had adapted English conventions to life on the frontier and borrowed others from their Native American neighbors. By the mid-1700s, life in colonial Massachusetts was uniquely American.

## The Colonial Home

This American—or "Yankee"—culture evolved from necessity. The first settlers of Massachusetts carved a home out of the land as best they could. The Pilgrims spent the first winter aboard the *Mayflower*, and families who settled the Massachusetts Bay Colony often lived in wigwams or dugouts until a house could be built. These first houses were usually one-room dwellings constructed of clapboard siding with thatched roofs and dirt floors. At the center of the home was a fireplace, used both for heating and for cooking. A stairway led to a sleeping loft above.

Over time, the colonists added on to these houses or replaced them with new, larger homes. A 1750 visitor to Salem, a fishing and shipbuilding community just north of Boston, reported that there were about 450 houses in the towns, "several of which are neat buildings, but all of wood . . . , being at a convenient distance from each other with fine gardens [at the] back."[23]

## Life on the Farm

Salem was urban compared with most towns in Massachusetts. Most people lived on farms beyond the town limits. Usually, farmers had several scattered parcels of land that they would put into cultivation at different times. This was inefficient because they had to spend time traveling between their tracts of land, bringing their farm equipment with them.

Early colonial homes in Massachusetts generally consisted of one large room and a sleeping loft.

The rocky soil and cold weather also made farming difficult. Only the hardiest crops survived. The colonists followed the example of the Native Americans and planted corn, squash, pumpkins, and beans. They also grew oats, rye, barley, cabbages, peas, turnips, and onions, as well as hay for the animals. They kept hens for their eggs, cows for their milk, and sheep for their wool, as well as cattle and pigs that would supply meat at special occasions. Sometimes fruit trees were also planted in orchards beyond the fields.

Farmers worked their own parcels of land, although they worked together during planting and harvesting. The austere conditions and inefficient use of land resulted in mostly subsistence farming. Throughout the colonial era, Massachusetts imported more food than it exported.

## Family Life

The typical eighteenth-century Massachusetts farm required the help of the entire family. The men performed the heavy farmwork, cleared the fields, and brought in the harvest. They worked together to build houses and other buildings. They also worked together to govern the community and plan for the future—only men were allowed to hold political office or vote.

Women were responsible for the home and family. They cooked the meals, kept the house clean, and made most of their families' clothes. The fancy clothes worn to church on Sunday might be made from fabrics imported from England, but most day-to-day clothes were made from flax, a plant that did well in the rocky Massachusetts soil. The women used spinning wheels to spin the flax into linen, which was then woven by hand on a loom and sewn into clothing. Like their Native American neighbors, the colonists also used deerskin and other animal pelts to make warm outerwear.

Even children were responsible for some of the chores. Girls learned housekeeping from their mothers while the boys helped their fathers in the fields.

## Education and Schools

When children weren't helping their parents, they were usually in school. The Puritans believed that it was important for everyone to

# First in Education

In most areas in the seventeenth century, children were schooled at home by their parents. The Puritans believed it was important for everyone to be able to read the Bible. In 1635, they founded Boston Latin Grammar School, the first public school in the New World. Just a year later, the College at Newtowne became the first school of higher education. The college was later named Harvard University.

In keeping with the priorities of the Puritans, Harvard was designed primarily to provide training for the ministry, but it offered a wide range of studies in literature, arts, and sciences. According to an early brochure published in 1643, Harvard was founded "To advance Learning and perpetuate it to Posterity; dreading to leave an illiterate Ministry to the Churches." In *Colonial Massachusetts,* Benjamin W. Labaree calls the founding of Harvard "a remarkable achievement for a frontier society, especially considering the fact that no other English colony undertook such an ambitious project at a comparative stage in its development."

The population's passion for reading resulted in a number of other firsts in Massachusetts: the first American printing press was set up in Cambridge by Stephen Daye in 1638, the first public library was founded in Boston in 1653, and the first regularly issued newspaper in America, the *Boston News-Letter,* was published in Boston in 1704.

be able to read the Bible, so they passed a law in 1647 that all towns with fifty or more households needed to have a school. The schools were supported through taxes. Usually, parents also paid a modest tuition, which was waived for those who could not afford it. "This system of state-supported, compulsory education was a sharp break with tradition," writes historian Jerome R. Reich. "Neither in England nor elsewhere on the American continent had education been considered a public function." [24] Yet, such laws became widespread in the colonies. Within a decade, all the other colonies in New England except Rhode Island had copied the Massachusetts law, with minor variations.

The first schools usually consisted of just one schoolmaster teaching all the children of the town at the same time, regardless of

Massachusetts was the first colony to make education available to all children.

their age. As towns became larger and more dispersed, schools rotated from one part of town to another to enable all students to attend at least some of the school year. This method proved inefficient. By the end of the colonial period, the towns in Massachusetts had divided themselves into school districts with taxing power to support their own schools.

Colonial schools in Massachusetts used catechisms and Bible stories to teach reading and writing. Studies for girls included reading and writing, and perhaps basic arithmetic. Girls also often learned practical skills such as sewing and knitting. Only boys attended grammar schools, where they studied Latin and Greek, and, by the end of the colonial period, modern languages, mathematics, science, history, and other subjects. A few went on to college—almost always Harvard, which had been founded near Boston in 1636.

The Puritans' emphasis on education set Massachusetts apart from other colonies. The literacy rate in Massachusetts at the end of the seventeenth century was about 90 percent for males and 50 percent for females, compared to only 60 percent and 25 percent, respectively, in Virginia.

# The New England Primer

*The* New England Primer, *first published in 1690, was used as the basic textbook to teach reading. The primer contained the Lord's Prayer and other prayers, the Ten Commandments, and other religious and moral teachings. The most famous part of the* New England Primer *is its rhymed alphabet, which featured not only the ABC's but also moral teachings.*

An excerpt from the *New England Primer*, which taught morality and the alphabet simultaneously.

**A**    In *Adam's* Fall We Sinned all.

**B**    Thy Life to Mend This *Book* Attend.

**C**    The *Cat* doth play And after flay.

**D**    A *Dog* will bite A Thief at night.

**E**    An *Eagles* flight Is out of fight.

**F**    The Idle *Fool* Is whipt at School.

## Towns and Villages

The school was one of several community buildings at the center of the typical Massachusetts town. In addition, there would usually be a general store, a blacksmith's shop, and other small businesses. These core buildings were built around an open tract of land called a "common" because everyone used it as common space, or a "green" because sheep and other animals often grazed there. Much of the land granted to the typical town was left as woods, where the colonists could obtain firewood and stones for building fences. One or two garrison houses were often built at the outer perimeter of the town to defend against Indian attacks. Most of the settlers lived on farms beyond the town limits.

Because farming was the primary occupation, the quest for new land to till was constant. Expanding the amount of land under the plow was the best way to increase one's wealth. As new immigrants came to Massachusetts, they, too, needed land on which to live. When one area got too crowded, groups of people would apply for a charter to establish a new town.

The Massachusetts legislature required townships to be granted only to groups of settlers, not to individuals or absentee landlords. Often, a group came together to ask for a charter for a town—not just to meet a need for more land, but also to establish a community in which they could worship and live as they pleased. Historian Kenneth A. Lockridge explains, "Within the limits set by the emerging policies of the colony,

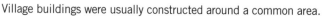

Village buildings were usually constructed around a common area.

groups of settlers everywhere were coalescing and searching for the opportunity to create a communal life, seeking to shape in their own agricultural villages their own versions of the good society." [25]

The town of Dedham, for example, was founded in 1636 by thirty men, many of whom were strangers to one another, who had come to Massachusetts during the Puritan migration. Like the Pilgrims, they signed a covenant agreeing to obey the rules made by the group. They also pledged to "practice one truth according to that most perfect rule, the foundation whereof is everlasting love." [26] Although they opened the community to newcomers, anyone moving to Dedham would have to sign the covenant.

Even in towns without covenants there was a strong sense of community and common purpose. Collective labor was needed to build roads and erect houses and other buildings. The harsh living conditions on the frontier further strengthened the communal bond among the colonists. New settlements were vulnerable to Indian attacks, and there was strength in numbers.

## Land Ownership

Setting up a town also required planning. Within very broad guidelines established by the colonial government, towns were given the authority to govern their own affairs. Locally elected leaders, called selectmen, settled a host of issues, ranging from where and what type of buildings could be built, how elections would be conducted, what taxes would be collected, and how public money would be spent. At the beginning, townspeople came together once a year to elect the selectmen. As time passed, towns began to hold additional meetings to discuss and vote on important issues. Through these town meetings, power gradually shifted from the selectmen to the general population.

The townspeople worked together to select the best site for the common and other communal space, and then divided up the remaining land to be parceled out among the members of the group. Usually, the parcels of land were allotted randomly, so that each family had several parcels spread throughout the area. This system helped to distribute the land fairly and equally, as no one person was likely to get all the best acreage. Douglas Leach writes:

From the beginning, one important principle established in the Bay Colony was that land should be held by individuals in free tenure as personal property, without the obligation of continuing payments to a landlord. . . . A second important ideal embedded in Massachusetts land policy was that landholding should be widespread among the population, that men should have land in amounts roughly proportional to their ability to make constructive use of it, and that engrossment of great tracts of land by ambitious individuals should be prevented.[27]

This system of land ownership contributed to a highly democratic way of life. Only men who owned property were allowed to participate in the town meetings or vote, but in Massachusetts,

In Massachusetts, land and homes were considered personal property, meaning residents were not beholden to a landlord.

property was divided among a relatively large number of people. "An outstanding feature of New England rural society," writes historian Richard Hofstadter, "was the relatively small proportion of landless men, which, even in the eastern Massachusetts counties, did not usually exceed 20 per cent." [28] As a result, an estimated three-quarters of the men in colonial Massachusetts—a much larger percentage than in other colonies—were eligible to vote.

## The Economy

Because most people owned property, the gap between the rich and the poor in Massachusetts was relatively small. "Striking as the social distance might be between a Boston or Newport merchant and the poorest of the inland villagers," writes Richard Hofstadter, "there was so little contrast between the rich and the poor. New Englanders had quite unwittingly devised an economy as close to egalitarian as anything in the Western world." [29]

Throughout the colonial period, most of the people remained farmers, but over time the economy gradually became increasingly diversified. Benjamin Labaree concludes, "The most significant change taking place in mid–eighteenth century Massachusetts was the gradual modernization of towns and villages from self-sufficient farming communities to complex societies increasingly dependent on the world around them." [30] Whaling, fishing, and shipbuilding created prosperous towns up and down the coast. Massachusetts merchants also capitalized on the colony's natural resources—the abundant animal life brought income for their furs, while the tall pine trees enabled a profitable living in timber.

To get the best price for its products, Massachusetts traded with countries in Europe and the West Indies. The other English colonies looked to Massachusetts to build ships—a profitable business due to the growing population in the Americas and the growing demand for goods from other places. Commerce thus brought Massachusetts closer to its colonial neighbors and to countries throughout the world.

By the end of the colonial period, Massachusetts had grown from a fledgling settlement to a comparatively wealthy colony with a large and strong middle class. In 1772, during a visit to Ireland, Benjamin Franklin compared the plight of the people there with that of New

Englanders. "I thought often of the happiness of New England," he wrote, "where every man is a freeholder, has a vote in public affairs, lives in a tidy warm house, has plenty of good food and fuel, with whole clothes from head to foot, the manufacture perhaps of his own family."[31]

## The Spirit of Massachusetts

Franklin's comparison between New England and Ireland shows how far Massachusetts had come. It was no longer a group of Englishmen living abroad—nor was it just another American colony. The Puritan ideal of community and commitment to forging a better life lived on in the hearts and minds of the colonists. The Puritans' commitment to education contributed to a literate and well-educated population. The autonomy of town government had given the Massachusetts colonists a belief in the right to self-government. And a burgeoning economy dependent on trade strengthened the colonists' resolve to protect their commercial interests against tyranny at home or abroad.

The Puritan beliefs in education and the strength of the community laid out the foundation for the Massachusetts colony's push for self-government.

Above all, the experiences of the Massachusetts colonists had taught them to fight for their beliefs. The Pilgrims and Puritans had fought the wilderness to carve out a better way of life. With Yankee independence, their descendants were prepared to fight to protect what they had built.

## Chapter Four

# The Revolutionary Spirit

The American Revolution was more than a war—it was a revolution in thought that began long before the first shot was fired. Looking back on the revolutionary experience in 1815, John Adams, a lawyer who had played an integral role in Massachusetts's resistance to British rule, asked, "What do we mean by the Revolution? The war? That was no part of the Revolution; it was only an effect and consequence of it. The Revolution was in the minds of the people, and this was effected, from 1760 to 1775, in the course of fifteen years before a drop of blood was shed at Lexington."[32] Massachusetts was at the center of this revolution in thought.

### An Era of Taxation

Massachusetts had already become known in England for its defiant spirit. Just as they had with the Navigation Acts several years earlier, the colonists of Massachusetts were among the leading forces in resisting the taxes that England levied on the colonists in the 1760s and 1770s.

England initiated the taxes to cover its debt. For the better part of a century, the mother country had engaged in a series of wars with France (collectively known as the French and Indian Wars) for control over the New World. The ongoing conflict had drained England's financial resources. Parliament reasoned that since the wars were fought to defend British colonists from French aggression and protect their trade rights, the colonies should bear a large portion of the cost.

The first revenue-generating measure was the Sugar Act of 1764, a tax that affected only the relatively wealthy merchants on the eastern shore of Massachusetts. The Stamp Act, which was passed just a year later, had a much broader effect. The act required colonists to buy and place revenue stamps on legal documents, newspapers, playing cards, and other printed items. In towns throughout the colony, people met to consider what could be done to put a halt to the taxes. John Adams wrote in his diary:

> The people, even to the lowest ranks, have become more attentive to their liberties and more determined to defend them than they were ever known to be. Our presses have groaned, our pulpits have thundered, our legislatures have resolved, our towns have voted.[33]

The Stamp Act, passed in 1765, required colonists to buy stamps like these and place them on most printed items.

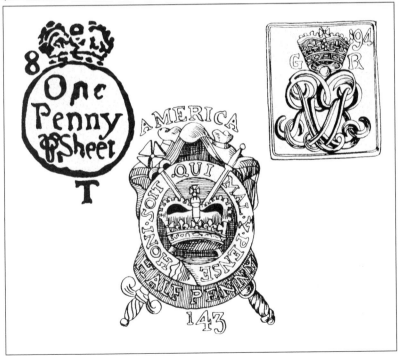

Recognizing that the resistance of Massachusetts alone would do little to curtail England, Massachusetts called for a meeting of all the colonies to consider how to stop the taxes. A Boston merchant named Sam Adams was among the organizers of the Stamp Act Congress, which became the first intercolonial assembly initiated by the colonists.

## No Taxation Without Representation

At the meeting, the colonial representatives resolved:

That it is inseparably essential to the freedom of a people, and the undoubted right of Englishmen, that no taxes be imposed on them, but with their own consent, given personally, or by their representatives. That the people of these colonies are not, and from their local circumstances cannot be, represented in the House of Commons in Great-Britain. That the only representatives of the people of these colonies, are persons chosen therein by themselves, and that no taxes ever have been, or can be constitutionally imposed on them, but by their respective legislatures.[34]

In short, there should be "no taxation without representation."

"No taxation without representation" became a rallying cry throughout Massachusetts. The colonists refused to use the stamps and circulated unstamped newspapers and pamphlets. Violence erupted in Boston as colonists clashed with stamp collectors. A group of rebels vandalized the home of Governor Thomas Hutchinson, who was seen as a supporter of England. Parliament repealed the Stamp Act just three months after its passage.

But the fight was far from over. Charles Townshend, Britain's chancellor, argued that England was unwise to give in to the colonists' pressure and repeal the Stamp Act. He proposed another way to raise revenues in the colonies. The resulting Townshend Acts imposed a series of duties on the import of glass, lead, paints, paper, and tea—all of which the Navigation Acts said could be purchased only from

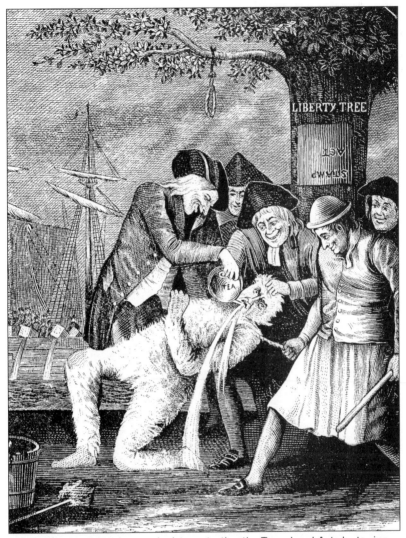

This political cartoon shows colonists protesting the Townshend Acts by tarring and feathering an English tax collector.

England. The Massachusetts colonists protested the legislation by boycotting some goods and smuggling others.

## Getting Organized

The colonists were also becoming organized in their opposition. Years of working together in town meetings and elected assemblies had given the Massachusetts statesmen an understanding of how to work together for the good of the community. In towns and villages throughout the colony, the colonists formed associations that declared their intention to resist England's taxes by any means necessary—or as they usually put it, "to the last extremity." [35] The best-known opposition group was Boston's Sons of Liberty, which Sam Adams had helped organize.

Also at Sam Adams's suggestion, the Massachusetts assembly established a formal committee to communicate information about Britain's attacks on colonial liberties. Other colonies soon followed suit. These Committees of Correspondence formed a core of patriots who were prepared to work together if there were any further violations of colonial rights.

Colonists organized in groups to resist England's taxes.

# On Sam Adams

*Samuel Adams, a native Bostonian, played a critical role during the events leading up to the American Revolution, leading the British to label him "the most dangerous man in Massachusetts." In* Origin & Progress of the American Rebellion, *British loyalist Peter Oliver blamed Sam Adams for much of what had occurred. A Tory painter, wrote Oliver, said that "if he wished to draw the Picture of the Devil…he would get Sam Adams to sit for him." In the following excerpt from* Colonial Massachusetts, *historian Benjamin W. Labaree discusses the influence of Sam Adams.*

The role played by Samuel Adams during the critical years from 1770 to 1774 has frequently been described as indispensable. Without Adams, many historians have seemed to say, there would have been no Revolution. Surely he contributed more during this period than any other individual … to the "perfect crisis" of 1774. But neither he nor anyone else was the indispensable man. "Pioneer in propaganda" he may have been, but that is not to say that he controlled the "mobs" of Boston, let alone the thousands of other inhabitants of Massachusetts. The people of the Bay colony could and did think for themselves. When the committee of correspondence sent around its Boston Pamphlet in 1772, for instance, it knew better than to suggest that other towns adopt the resolutions as their own. When numerous communities did respond, they discussed the issues first in town meeting and then expressed their conclusions in their own language.…And yet…Adams had the knack, as he so well demonstrated … of inspiring others to express the views they shared in common with so many inhabitants of Massachusetts. By so doing he encouraged them to make a commitment, not only in words but in deeds as well. As a result, by 1774 he stood at the head not of a mob of blind automatons but of an army of well-informed freemen.

Thanks in part to the alliances among like-minded colonists, news of the Townshend Acts spread quickly. A torrent of newspaper editorials, pamphlets, and other documents proclaimed that Parliament was trampling the rights of the colonists. Again, the colonists agreed to a boycott of the taxed items. Parliament considered repealing the legislation but did not want it to look like England was again backing down because of American resistance. In 1770, the British leaders decided the best solution was to repeal all the measures except one: a tax on tea "to keep up the right,"[36] as the British chief minister put it.

## The Boston Massacre

Meanwhile in Boston, another event took place to further turn public opinion against England. Since the French and Indian Wars, Britain had stationed troops in Boston to keep the peace. As the colonists became angry with British rule, they regularly harassed the soldiers with jeers, insults, and occasionally with snowballs or rocks.

The 1770 Boston Massacre infuriated Massachusetts colonists.

On March 5, 1770, a group of Bostonians began picking on the lone sentry standing guard in front of the customhouse. Some people threw ice and rocks at the sentry and threatened to kill him. A group of British soldiers rushed out to defend the man from the crowd, which numbered at least three hundred and seemed to be growing by the minute. They had formed a line around the sentry when a gun suddenly went off accidentally. Thinking that an order to fire had been given, the soldiers shot into the crowd, killing five people and wounding several more.

Boston patriots took advantage of this calamity. Eyewitness accounts were compiled into "A Short Narrative of the Horrid Massacre in Boston," and Paul Revere, a Boston silversmith, engraved a scene of British soldiers firing on an unarmed crowd. The Boston Massacre, as the incident quickly became known, would not soon be forgotten. "Americans had always been suspicious of standing armies," writes historian Benjamin W. Labaree, "and . . . the use of military force against civilians had long ranked high as an indication of governmental tyranny. Succeeding anniversaries of the Massacre were marked with ringing reminders from public orators and writers of the horrors of standing armies." [37]

## The Boston Tea Party

England was conciliatory. It brought the soldiers responsible for firing on the colonists to trial and removed its remaining troops from Boston. With the withdrawal of British troops and the repeal of the Townshend Acts, the colonies entered a period of relative stability. But the calm would be short-lived. Just three years later, tea would rekindle the fire.

The events began with the passage of the Tea Act in May 1773. Designed to help the British East India Company unload its surplus tea, the Tea Act lowered England's tax on tea and allowed the company to distribute tea directly to colonial retailers, bypassing American colonial merchants. This would lower the price of the tea, so that the East India Company would be able to undercut the price of the Dutch tea that was being smuggled into the colonies.

The colonists saw the Tea Act as a way to trick them into buying from England and paying the tax. They wanted no part of the East India Company tea, no matter how cheaply it came. New York and Philadelphia sent the ships carrying tea back to England, but the royal

# John Adams

John Adams, Samuel Adams's cousin, would also play an integral role in the events leading up to and following the American Revolution. Born in Braintree, Adams graduated from Harvard College in 1755 and went on to practice law. In 1770, Adams took on the defense of the British soldiers tried for the Boston Massacre and successfully won acquittals for seven of the defendants and reduced sentences of manslaughter for the remaining two.

As a representative at the Continental Congress from 1774 to 1777, Adams became an outspoken advocate of independence and was appointed to the committee to draft a declaration of independence in 1776. Adams also drafted the state constitution of Massachusetts, which is still in effect today. As the Revolutionary War waged in the Americas, Adams served as a diplomat in France, where he helped convince that country to join the colonies' bid for freedom. He was instrumental in brokering peace between the newly created United States and Great Britain in the Treaty of Paris.

Adams was elected the first vice president and the second president of the United States.

governor of Massachusetts refused to allow the ships in Boston Harbor to leave. On December 16, a group of Bostonians disguised as Mohawk Indians stole onto the tea ships and dumped overboard forty-five tons of tea.

The event showed how far the colonists had come in their opposition to British rule. Unlike most of the events that the colonists had staged previously, the "Boston Tea Party" was a well-planned, premeditated act of rebellion. "All Things were conducted with great order, Decency, and perfect submission to government," wrote John Adams in a letter to a colleague. "The dye is cast: The People have passed the River and cutt away the Bridge: . . . This is the grandest Event, which has ever yet happened."[38] The Boston Tea Party put Boston at the forefront of the colonial resistance to British rule.

## Parliament Ups the Ante

England refused to consider retreat or compromise. Instead, Parliament passed measures intended to isolate Massachusetts and scare the more moderate colonies into obedience. England demanded compensation for the lost tea and closed the port of Boston until the debt was paid. It also curtailed the powers of Massachusetts's colonial representative assemblies, granting broad new powers to the royal governor and stripping the right of the representative assembly to elect the governor's council. Richard D. Brown sums up, "In a single statute the ministry . . . attempted to terminate the system of responsible government by consent that the inhabitants [of Massachusetts] had developed over generations."[39]

The legislation backfired: instead of turning away from Massachusetts as Britain had hoped, the colonists elsewhere were outraged. In September 1774, fifty-five delegates from twelve of the thirteen colonies met at the First Continental Congress in Philadelphia. They declared England's actions—which they called the "Intolerable Acts"—to be unconstitutional and destructive to the freedom of the colonists and reiterated that Parliament had no power to tax the colonists without their consent. They resolved to boycott all trade with England—exports as well as imports. Donations of food, clothing, and money flooded into Boston from throughout the colonies to help the merchants who were hurt by the closing of the Boston port.

## The "Shot Heard 'Round the World"

In Massachusetts, the colonists, stockpiling arms and ammunition, prepared to put might behind their actions. They had always had local militia units to defend against Indian attacks; now these militias prepared to fight against England. Because they were trained to be up and ready at a moment's notice, they became known as minutemen.

In April 1775, England learned about a cache of arms in Concord and sent troops to collect the weapons. The minutemen were ready for them. Forewarned by Paul Revere in his famous ride, about seventy men gathered on Lexington's green to meet the British soldiers. Realizing that they were far outnumbered by the British, the colonists began to disperse. Suddenly, a shot rang out, and a barrage of bullets followed. Within minutes, eight Americans lay dead and another ten wounded. It was never established who fired what poet Ralph Waldo Emerson later called the "shot heard 'round the world" that marked the beginning of the American Revolution.

The British continued their march on to Concord, but word about the events at Lexington preceded them. When the troops reached Concord, the minutemen converged on a small platoon and forced them to turn back. Colonists continued to fire upon the British as they made their way back to Boston. By the time the British reached Boston, British casualties numbered more than 270; American casualties were fewer than 100.

## The Battle of Bunker Hill

As the British soldiers regrouped in Boston, colonists from all over Massachusetts and neighboring colonies settled just outside the town to prepare for England's next move. When the Americans heard that the British planned to strengthen their position by gaining control of

The Revolutionary War began in April 1775 when British soldiers and Massachusetts minutemen clashed on the green of Lexington.

Minutemen throughout New England were prepared to aid the Massachusetts colonists.

the hills in Charlestown (now part of Boston), they decided to get there first.

Colonel William Prescott planned to establish fortifications on Bunker Hill but decided at the last minute that Breed's Hill would be more advantageous. On June 17, 1775, the two sides prepared for battle. As the Americans built fortifications on Breed's Hill, twenty-five hundred British troops marched across the Charles River toward them. As they advanced, Prescott reportedly instructed the colonists to hold their fire on the soldiers "until you see the whites of their eyes."

The Americans did as instructed. They waited until the British were within fifty feet before opening fire. The British had no choice but to retreat, leaving behind hundreds of fallen soldiers. It took three assaults to chase away the undermanned and poorly armed

One of the bloodiest battles of the Revolution, the Battle of Bunker Hill, resulted in the killing and wounding of one thousand British soldiers and four hundred colonists.

American troops. The Battle of Bunker Hill, which was actually fought on Breed's Hill, marked the first real battle of the Revolutionary War—and would be among the bloodiest. More than one thousand British soldiers and about four hundred Americans were killed or wounded.

## Independence at Last

The minutemen of Massachusetts had been joined by the militia of several other New England colonies in the Battle of Bunker Hill. However, the delegates to the Continental Congress meeting in Philadelphia realized that victory against the powerful British army would require a coordinated effort of all the colonies. Therefore, Congress agreed to create the Continental army on June 14, 1775. John Adams rose to nominate Virginian George Washington as its commander in chief—a nomination that met with resounding approval. Two weeks later, Washington arrived in Massachusetts to take over control of the colonial militia. The war was no longer between England and *one* of her colonies—it was between England

and *all* of her colonies. The following spring, Washington and the colonial militia drove the British out of Boston.

Meanwhile, the Second Continental Congress was meeting in Philadelphia to determine the appropriate course of action. John Adams and Sam Adams were among the Massachusetts delegates. The cousins were vocal in arguing that there was no recourse but to separate from England, and as the events unfolded in Massachusetts, more and more delegates agreed with them.

Although the Massachusetts representatives were anxious for independence from England, they realized that it was important for other states to take the lead. In particular, they wanted strong support from Virginia, a large, powerful colony that would help garner support among its southern neighbors. When a committee of five people was appointed to draft a declaration of independence, John Adams insisted that Thomas Jefferson, a young lawyer from Virginia, write the draft.

## The Need for a New Government

When the Declaration of Independence was signed on July 4, 1776, the thirteen colonies proclaimed that they would no longer be governed by England. The question remained, however, of how they would be governed. In Massachusetts, the charter of 1691, which had provided the system of government for decades, was no longer applicable. John Adams later wrote in his autobiography, "I always expected we should have more difficulty and danger in our attempts to govern ourselves ..., than from all the fleets and armies of Great Britain."[40]

Virginia drafted a state constitution to replace its current charter late in 1776. In the next few years, one colony after another followed suit. However, when the Massachusetts legislature suggested in 1776 that it, too, should draft a state constitution, citizens rejected the idea. "If the towns replying to the General Court ... agreed on nothing else," explains historian Benjamin Labaree, "almost all of them strongly believed that the people, voting through their town meetings, should at least have the right to review any proposed constitution."[41]

The Massachusetts House of Representatives tried again in 1778. This time, they drew up a constitution and voted on its approval before

# John Adams Plans for Self-Government

*Even before the Declaration of Independence, John Adams was planning for a new government. He was instrumental in encouraging the states to draft constitutions between 1776 and 1780. His sense of optimism is clear in this excerpt from a letter written in January 1776, taken from Winthrop D. Jordan and Leon F. Littwack's, The United States.*

As politics is the art of securing human happiness, and the prosperity of societies depends upon the constitution of government under which they live, there cannot be a more agreeable employment to a benevolent mind than the study of the best kinds of government.

It has been the will of Heaven that we should be thrown into existence at a period when the greatest philosophers and lawgivers of antiquity would have wished to live. A period when a coincidence of circumstances without example, has afforded to thirteen Colonies, at once, an opportunity of beginning government anew from the foundation, and building as they choose. How few of the human race have ever had any opportunity of choosing a system of government for themselves and their children! How few have ever had any thing more of choice in government than in climate! These Colonies have now their election; and it is much to be wished that it may not prove to be like a prize in the hands of a man who has no heart to improve it.

sending it on to the towns. Once again, the citizens turned it down. They believed the people, not the legislature, should decide what their government should look like. Historian Edmund S. Morgan explains:

[The citizens of Massachusetts] had decided that the people should endow the government with a constitution and not vice versa. If, they reasoned, a government can make its own constitution, the government can change it and thus fall into tyranny.[42]

Finally, in September 1779, a convention was called to write a new constitution. Thirty delegates from throughout the state spent seven months creating a system of government for Massachusetts. John Adams drew up the first draft.

Adams was well suited to the task. He had spent considerable time studying modern political theories. He had carefully considered how the ideal of self-government might be practiced in a republic. Richard D. Brown explains, "Drawing on the most enlightened political science of the day and on Whig ideals, Adams designed a modern governing structure that enshrined the traditional ideals of the Bay Colony."[43]

## Massachusetts Becomes a State

The constitution Adams wrote began with a preamble that said that the purpose of government is "to secure the existence of the body-politic; and to furnish the individuals who compose it, with . . . their natural rights and the blessings of life."[44] A declaration of "natural, essential, and unalienable rights" followed. These included free elections, equal protection of the laws, trial by jury, freedom from unreasonable search and seizure, a free press, free assembly and petition, and the right to bear arms. In part at Massachusetts's urging, all of these rights would later be incorporated into the U.S. Bill of Rights.

The convention finished its work on the constitution in March 1780 and sent it on to the towns for ratification. One by one, the towns held their ratifying conventions, where a "querulous individualism marked the evaluation of the document."[45] In the end, however, the people of Massachusetts—through their town governments—approved the document. An election for governor was quickly called, and John Hancock, a Boston merchant who had emerged as a leader in the revolutionary cause, was elected the new state's first governor.

## Independence at Last

The first task of the new Massachusetts government was to help defeat the British. In the end, it would take almost eight long years and the loss of many lives before England would concede to give up its colonies. Like the other colonies, Massachusetts provided men, money, and supplies to support the war effort, but after the Battle of Bunker Hill, the war was waged beyond Massachusetts's boundaries.

Finally, on October 19, 1781, the British surrendered after Washington launched a surprise attack on Yorktown, Virginia. This was the last major battle of the American Revolution. With the signing of the Treaty of Paris two years later, England ceded the new United States its land in the New World. Massachusetts was part of a new nation.

## Chapter Five

# Early Statehood and Beyond

Freed from the reins of England, the thirteen fledgling states struggled to find a way to work together. During the Revolutionary War, although the new Americans were wary of creating a system of government that would have power over all the colonies, they had recognized the need to work together to defeat England. They had drafted a document that bound the states together in a "firm league of friendship." These Articles of Confederation allowed the states to remain independent sovereignties but provided for a common army with members raised and paid for by individual states.

With England's defeat, however, the Articles of Confederation soon proved inadequate. Nowhere were its shortcomings more apparent than in Massachusetts. As Massachusetts struggled to establish its place in the new world order, it became apparent just how far its citizens had come in their self-assurance and their quest for self-government.

### The Economy

One of the effects of the American Revolution had been a disturbance of the economy. Many merchants had profited during the war by selling ships and wartime supplies to neighboring colonies. Furthermore, as Tories—colonists who had supported Britain—fled

Boston and the surrounding towns, they left behind valuable property and businesses that were gobbled up by others left behind.

Thomas Treat Paine, a Massachusetts delegate to the Continental Congress, wrote in a letter to fellow statesman Elbridge Gerry that "the course of war has thrown property into channels, where before, it never was, and has increased little streams to overflowing rivers: and what is worse, in some respects by a method that has drained the sources of some as much as it has replenished others." [46]

In short, the interests of merchants, located mostly along the eastern seaboard, differed from those of the largely subsistence farmers living in the western part of the state. During the war, the two groups had found common ground in defeating England, but events at the end of the war exaggerated their differences.

## Issues of Representation

Among the most divisive issues was representation in the new Massachusetts government. In drafting the state constitution, a compromise had been reached: the upper house of the legislature (the senate) would be apportioned according to tax districts, and the lower house would comprise at least one representative from every incorporated town according to a formula that gave larger towns more representatives but not in proportion to their size. In an effort to appease westerners who complained about the cost of travel for their delegates, the Massachusetts legislature paid travel costs (one round-trip each session) for all delegates.

Although the western towns submitted to this system of representation, they remained somewhat alienated from the legislative system. Richard D. Brown explains:

> Hampshire and Berkshire [Counties] had never been thoroughly integrated into provincial or state politics due largely to geography. Patterns of trade and settlement in the west ran north and south along the river valleys, connecting the area almost as closely to Connecticut as to Massachusetts. During the colonial era government patronage had tied county notables to the royal government, within the western towns people had typically deferred to the leadership of the regional

The Massachusetts state constitution solved the problem of representation with a compromise: members of the state senate were appointed while the lower house allotted members based on town populations.

elite. But the Revolution disrupted both of these sources of cohesion, so social and economic tensions came to focus on the shortcomings of state fiscal policy, a policy that more nearly met the needs of eastern merchants and tradesmen than of farmers who were semi-self-sufficient.[47]

The people of western Massachusetts were suspicious of their neighbors to the east, and many were resentful of their relative prosperity. As a result of the long battle for independence, the Massachusetts townspeople had become fervent in their belief in self-government and their right to representation.

## Depression Brings Rebellion

The end of the Revolutionary War and the shift in the economy brought on a severe depression in Massachusetts—a depression that hit farmers particularly hard. Most of the farmers in western Massachusetts were poor, and many owed a substantial amount of money because of liens on their land. Under the laws in effect at that time, debtors were imprisoned and their land was confiscated.

Late in the summer of 1786, delegates from fifty towns in Hampshire County met to compile a list of grievances. The seventeen complaints included issues related to the systems of taxation, elections, and representation. They believed the state's fiscal policy was being mismanaged and questioned the authority of the courts to foreclose on their property. The delegates demanded that a special legislative session be held to revise the constitution.

Although the delegates urged restraint, the townspeople's anger was not easily curbed. A week after the Hampshire County meeting, over a thousand armed men seized the courthouse in Northampton, and less than a month later, several hundred stopped the court in Worcester from meeting. Another several hundred men, led by Daniel Shays, a farmer who had served as captain during the American Revolution, attempted to take over the state supreme court in Springfield. Massachusetts responded with a show of force that seemed to put an end to mob rule, but Shays gathered a force of more than a thousand men to lead a raid on a nearby federal arsenal.

This event, which became known as Shays's Rebellion was quelled in a matter of days, but it caused alarm throughout the states and pointed out inadequacies of the existing national government. Massachusetts's call for federal help in suppressing the uprising went unanswered. Throughout the colonies, people used what had occurred in Massachusetts as proof that a stronger central government was needed to maintain order and to handle the economy.

## Moving Beyond the Articles

Supporters of a stronger central government used Shays's Rebellion as a rallying cry. In 1787, Massachusetts joined eleven other states (Rhode Island declined to participate) at a meeting in Philadelphia "to take into consideration the situation of the United States, to devise such further provisions as shall appear to them necessary to render the constitution of the Federal Government adequate to the exigencies of the Union."[48] The meeting was called the "Grand Convention" or

In 1786, Daniel Shays led a mob to overtake government buildings; his rebellion emphasized the need for a stronger central government.

# A Crisis of Authority

*Reacting to Shays's Rebellion, the* American Recorder, *a Charlestown, Massachusetts, newspaper, published an editorial on March 16, 1787, arguing that events demonstrated the need for a stronger national government. This excerpt is taken from William Dudley's* The Creation of the Constitution.

This is a crisis in our affairs, which requires all the wisdom and energy of government; for every man of sense must be convinced that our disturbances have arisen, more from a want of power, than the abuse of it—from the relaxation, and almost annihilation of our federal government—from the feeble, unsystematic, temporising, inconstant character of our own state—from the derangement of our finances—the oppressive absurdity of our mode of taxation—and from the astonishing enthusiasm and perversion of principles among the people. It is not extraordinary that commotions have been excited. It is strange, that under the circumstances which we have been discussing, that they did not appear sooner, and terminate more fatally. For let it be remarked, that a feeble government produces more factions than an oppressive one. The want of power first makes individuals pretended legislators, and then, active rebels. Where parents want authority, children are wanting in duty. It is not possible to advance further in the same path. Here the ways divide, the one will conduct us to anarchy, and next to foreign or domestic tyranny: the other, by the wise and vigorous exertion of lawful authority, will lead to permanent power, and general prosperity. I am no advocate for despotism; but I believe the probability to be much less of its being introduced by the corruption of our rules, than by the delusion of the people....

While the bands of union are so loose, we are no more entitled to the character of a nation than the hordes of vagabond traitors. Reason has ever condemned our paltry prejudices upon this important subject. Now that experience has come in aid of reason, let us renounce them. For what is there now to prevent our subjugation by a foreign power, but their contempt of the acquisition? It is time to render the federal head supreme in the United States.

"Federal Convention" at the time. When the delegates turned their attention to writing a new constitution for the United States, the meeting became better known as the Constitutional Convention.

Massachusetts sent four delegates to the convention: Elbridge Gerry, Nathaniel Gorham, Rufus King, and Caleb Strong. Each of these men had experience in the colonial legislature, state legislature, or both. Elbridge Gerry had been influential during Massachusetts's struggle against England; Nathaniel Gorham had served as the president of the Continental Congress.

The Massachusetts delegates brought their experiences to bear on the debates in Philadelphia, sharing the lessons they learned in politics and in drafting the state constitution. In *The Signers of the Constitution*, Robert G. Ferris and James H. Charleton write of Rufus King's influence on the proceedings:

At age 32, King was not only one of the most youthful of the delegates at Philadelphia, but was also one of the most

In 1787, fifty-five delegates met in Philadelphia to revise the Articles of Confederation. The result was a new U.S. Constitution.

important. He numbered among the most capable orators. Furthermore, he attended every session. Although he came to the Convention unconvinced that major changes should be made in the Articles of Confederation, during the debates his views underwent a startling transformation. [49]

Although John Adams was in London, he, too, influenced the proceedings. His new book, *A Defence of the Constitutions of Government of the United States of America*, was widely distributed among the delegates.

Perhaps the greatest contribution of Massachusetts was the method by which the U.S. Constitution was created and ratified. Only Massachusetts had gone through the cycle of calling a constitutional convention and then putting forth the resulting Constitution to the people for ratification. "Nevertheless," writes author Jerome R. Reich, "the tradition was established and gradually became an integral part of the American political procedure." [50] Unlike the Articles of Confederation, which required unanimous consent of all thirteen states to go into effect, the Constitution would become law upon the approval of nine state ratifying conventions.

## Opposition to the Constitution

Not everyone agreed that the strong central government proposed by the convention was a good idea. Elbridge Gerry was among the few delegates to the Constitutional Convention who declined to sign the document, stating that he advocated more moderate change. He worried that the proposed Constitution might provoke civil war between supporters of a strong central government and those who feared it, as had almost happened during Shays's Rebellion. Since Caleb Strong had been called home before the end of the convention, Nathaniel Gorham and Rufus King were the only signers from Massachusetts.

Gerry's sentiments reflected the general mood of the Massachusetts people. The citizens of Massachusetts did not like the idea of taking power away from the town meeting and putting it in the hands of representatives meeting far from home.

Among these Antifederalists, as they became known, were several revolutionary heroes. In addition to Elbridge Gerry, Sam Adams, and John

# "They Will Swallow Us Up"

*In Massachusetts, the debate about whether to ratify the U.S. Constitution often became heated. The views of Amos Singeltary, a farmer who had lived through the American Revolution, as presented in this excerpt, are characteristic of Massachusettsians. His mistrust of the people in favor of the Constitution is evident in this excerpt from* The Spirit of 1787 *by Milton Lomask.*

Some gentlemen have called on them that were on the stage in the beginning of our troubles, in the year 1775. I was one of them. And I say that if anybody had proposed such a Constitution as this in that day, it would have been thrown away at once. It would not have been looked at.... Does not this Constitution take away all we have—all our property? Does it not lay all taxes, duties, imposts, and excises? And what more have we to give? ...

These lawyers and men of learning, and moneyed men that talk so finely, and gloss over matters too smoothly, to make us poor illiterate people swallow down the pill, expect to get into Congress themselves. They expect to be the managers of this Constitution, and get all the power and all the money into their own hands. And then they will swallow up us little fellows ... just as the whale swallowed up Jonah.

Hancock were among the leaders who engaged in the spirited debates that took place in the press as the Antifederalists listed their objections to the Constitution and the system of government it proposed.

The Antifederalists questioned whether it was wise to have representatives serve two- and six-year terms rather than being elected annually as was done in Massachusetts. They worried that there were no property or religious requirements for those who held national office. They feared having a representative body with the power to tax so far from home. Most of all, they worried about the Constitution's lack of a bill of rights.

## The Ratifying Convention

Early in 1788, when Massachusetts held a convention to decide whether or not to ratify the proposed Constitution, 355 delegates crowded into the statehouse, making it by far the largest ratifying convention. Supporters of the Constitution—or Federalists—were not optimistic about their chances of winning support. By their estimates, a majority of the delegates were against ratification.

The Federalist representatives at the Massachusetts convention were experienced and well-respected leaders, however. Among them were Rufus King, Nathaniel Gorham, and Caleb Strong. Elbridge Gerry, the fourth member of the Massachusetts delegation at the Constitutional Convention, was not elected to the convention.

Had it not been for the strong leadership and persuasive rhetoric of the Federalists, the Massachusetts convention would likely have voted against ratification. But after several days of debate in which each clause was dissected and discussed, many of the delegates who had been against the Constitution were persuaded of its merits. Most important, Sam Adams and John Hancock decided to support ratification, in part because of the commercial safeguards that a national government could provide.

Still bothered by the lack of a bill of rights, John Hancock rose to suggest a compromise: ratify the Constitution as it is now, with the proposal that a bill of rights be added immediately. Sam Adams seconded the idea. "A proposal of this sort, coming from Massachusetts," he said, "will have its weight."[51] On February 6, 1788, by a close vote (187 to 168), Massachusetts became the sixth state to ratify the Constitution. Several other states followed Massachusetts's example, ratifying the constitution with an accompanying proposed bill of rights.

Sam Adams strongly supported a bill of rights.

## Social Changes in the New State

The Massachusetts statesmen led the way in protecting their freedoms with a bill of rights because the experiences of the

# The Puritan Influence

*Puritan values are reflected in many aspects of American life today. Alan Simpson describes the lasting influence of the Puritans on politics in the last essay of* Puritanism in Old and New England.

In conclusion, let us return to the Puritan's impact on politics. Among his virtues I would list:

1. *His contribution to our system of limited government.*—The original Puritans had a genuine basis for their distrust of arbitrary power in addition to their experience of arbitrary government. They thought that man was too sinful to be trusted with too much power.... The Puritan tradition, with its everlasting insistence that only God is worthy of worship, is one insurance among Anglo-Saxon people that the state has no claim to worship.... They have defended, in season and out of season, the right to preach, to criticize, and to judge....

2. *His contribution to self-government—to the development of initiative and self-reliance in the body of the community.*—The Puritan pilgrimage has been a perpetual pilgrimage in self-help. The significance of the dissenting chapel as a training ground for working-class leadership...has often been emphasized....Nor should we forget ...the direct transfer from church affairs to political affairs of certain techniques of action....

3. *His contribution to education.*—...The most intellectual Puritans, in their desire to promote saving knowledge, have thrown up academy after academy, college after college, until their influence has been writ large over the history of education in England and America.

4. *His contribution to morality.*—The Puritan code has its repellent features, but it is no bad thing to have habits of honesty, sobriety, responsibility, and hard work impressed on a community.

Massachusetts colonists had instilled a fierce independence among its people. Generations after the Puritans first set foot in the New World, their values lived on in Massachusetts. The people of the new state believed it was important for their leaders to be godly and virtuous people. The state constitution made it mandatory for people who held public office to own property and to be members of a church. Over time, however, the citizens of Massachusetts learned to be more tolerant of other faiths and religions.

The firm belief in the rights of the people became evident when the issue of slavery came to the forefront in Massachusetts. Although slavery was not widely practiced in Massachusetts, there were no laws against owning or trading slaves. Many people believed that the institution of slavery was inconsistent with the ideals of the Declaration of Independence. In fact, the Massachusetts Constitution of 1780 also had declared in its first article, "All men are born free and equal." In 1783, the courts determined that this included men of all races, and Massachusetts became the first state in the union to outlaw slavery.

## The Spirit of Massachusetts

More than three centuries after the first Englishmen arrived in the New World, their spirit lives on. The reconstruction of Plymouth Plantation, the monuments at Lexington and Concord, and Faneuil Hall, where the colonists met to set up their new government—all are constant reminders of the critical role the people of Massachusetts played in forging the nation.

# Notes

## Introduction: The Bay State
1. Benjamin W. Labaree, *Colonial Massachusetts: A History*. Millwood, NY: KTO Press, 1979, pp. xv–xvi.

## Chapter One: In the Beginning
2. Quoted in Douglas Edward Leach, *The Northern Colonial Frontier, 1607–1763*. New York: Holt, Rinehart & Winston, 1966, p. 7.
3. Richard D. Brown, *Massachusetts*. New York: W. W. Norton, 1978, p. 10.
4. Leach, *Northern Colonial Frontier*, p. 2.
5. Quoted in Labaree, *Colonial Massachusetts*, p. 22.
6. Quoted in Richard Middleton, *Colonial America: A History, 1607–1760*. Cambridge, MA: Blackwell, 1992, p. 14.
7. Quoted in Oscar and Lilian Handlin, *Liberty and Power: 1600–1760*, New York: Harper & Row, 1986, p. 58.
8. Quoted in Francis Newton Thorpe, *The Federal and State Constitutions, Colonial Charters, and Other Organic Laws of the States, Territories, and Colonies Now or Heretofore Forming the United States of America*. Washington, DC: Government Printing Office, 1909.
9. Leach, *Northern Colonial Frontier*, p. 17.

## Chapter Two: The First Settlers
10. William Bradford, *Of Plimouth Plantation*. New York: Paragon Books, 1962, p. 59.
11. Bradford, *Of Plimouth Plantation*, p. 73.
12. Quoted in Leach, *Northern Colonial Frontier*, p. 18.
13. Bradford, *Of Plimouth Plantation*, p. 90.
14. Leach, *Northern Colonial Frontier*, p. 20.
15. John Winthrop, "A Modell of Christian Charity," written for the Massachusetts Bay Colony, 1630, as quoted on www.libertynet.org/~edcivic/winthrop.html. (Spelling in the quotation has been modernized.)

16. Edwin Tunis, *Colonial Living*. New York: Thomas Y. Crowell, 1957, pages 24–25.
17. Middleton, *Colonial America*, p. 79.
18. Leach, *Northern Colonial Frontier*, p. 19.
19. Jill Maynard, ed., *Through Indian Eyes: The Untold Story of Native American Peoples*. Pleasantville, NY: Reader's Digest, 1995, p. 137.
20. Labaree, *Colonial Massachusetts*, p. 105.
21. Samuel Eliot Morison, *The Maritime History of Massachusetts 1783–1860*. Boston: Houghton Mifflin, 1941, p. 27.

## Chapter Three: Life in Colonial Massachusetts

22. Richard Hofstadter, *America at 1750: A Social Portrait*. New York: Random House, 1973, p. 17.
23. Quoted in Labaree, *Colonial Massachusetts*, p. 159.
24. Jerome R. Reich, *Colonial America*, 4th ed. Upper Saddle River, NJ: Prentice-Hall, 1998, p. 227.
25. Kenneth A. Lockridge, *A New England Town: The First Hundred Years*. New York: W. W. Norton, 1970, p. 3.
26. Lockridge, *A New England Town*, pp. 4–5.
27. Leach, *Northern Colonial Frontier*, p. 44.
28. Hofstadter, *America at 1750*, p. 146.
29. Hofstadter, *America at 1750*, p. 143.
30. Labaree, *Colonial Massachusetts*, p. 165.
31. Quoted in Hofstadter, *America at 1750*, pp. 143–44.

## Chapter Four: The Revolutionary Spirit

32. Quoted in Hugh Brogan, *The Penguin History of the United States of America*. New York: Penguin Books, 1990, p. 138.
33. Quoted in Frank M. Fahey and Marie L. Fahey, *Chapters from the American Experience*. Vol. 1. Englewood Cliffs, NJ: Prentice-Hall, 1971, p. 130.
34. Quoted from Department of Humanities Computing, University of Groningen, "Resolutions of the Stamp Act Congress." Text prepared for "The American Revolution: An HTML Project," 1997. www.let.rug.nl/~usa/D/1751-1775/stampact/sa.htm.
35. Edmund S. Morgan, *The Birth of the Republic: 1763–89*. Chicago: University of Chicago Press, 1977, p. 22.
36. Quoted in Labaree, *Colonial Massachusetts*, p. 238.
37. Labaree, *Colonial Massachusetts*, p. 250.

38. Quoted in Brown, *Massachusetts*, p. 88.

39. Brown, *Massachusetts*, p. 90.

40. Quoted in Labaree, *Colonial Massachusetts*, p. 290.

41. Labaree, *Colonial Massachusetts*, p. 303.

42. Morgan, *Birth of the Republic*, p. 90.

43. Brown, *Massachusetts*, p. 108.

44. Quoted in Brown, *Massachusetts*, p. 108.

45. Brown, *Massachusetts*, p. 112.

## Chapter Five: Early Statehood and Beyond

46. Quoted in Brown, *Massachusetts*, pp. 104–105.

47. Brown, *Massachusetts*, p. 115.

48. Quoted in James MacGregor Burns, J. W. Peltason, Thomas E. Cronin, and David B. Magleby, *Government by the People.* 16th ed. Englewood Cliffs, NJ: Prentice-Hall, 1995, p. 13.

49. Robert G. Ferris and James H. Charleton, *The Signers of the Constitution.* Flagstaff, AZ: Interpretive Publications, 1986, p. 181.

50. Reich, *Colonial America*, p. 305.

51. Quoted in Catherine Drinker Bowen, *Miracle at Philadelphia.* Boston: Little, Brown, 1986, p. 289.

# Chronology

**1620**
The Pilgrims found the Plimouth Colony, Massachusetts's first permanent colony and the second permanent settlement in the British New World.

**1630**
English Puritans found the town of Boston, Massachusetts.

**1635**
Boston Latin Grammar School, the first public school in the colonies, is founded.

**1636**
The first college in the colonies is founded in present-day Cambridge; two years later it is renamed Harvard College after Puritan John Harvard leaves the college his books and a portion of his estate.

**1636**
Roger Williams is expelled from Massachusetts and founds Providence (Rhode Island).

**1647**
The Massachusetts Bay Colony passes a law requiring all towns with at least fifty inhabitants to have a school, thereby establishing the first public school system in the colonies.

**1675–1676**
King Philip's War takes place between English settlers and Native Americans in Massachusetts and neighboring colonies.

**1689–1697**
The first of a series of conflicts known as the French and Indian Wars, is waged between England and France.

**1691**
Massachusetts Bay Colony and Plymouth Colony are merged; the new Colony of Massachusetts's charter makes it a royal colony with a representative house.

**1704**
The *Boston News-Letter*, the first newspaper in the colonies, is founded at Cambridge.

**1735**
John Adams is born in Quincy.

**1754–1763**
The final French and Indian War (known as the Seven Years' War in Europe) is waged between England and France. England defeats France but is left with mounting war debt.

**1764**
Parliament passes the Sugar Act to raise money in the colonies.

**1765**
Parliament passes the Stamp Act; colonists come together at the Stamp Act Congress to discuss resistance.

**1766**
Parliament repeals the Stamp Act.

**1770**
British soldiers fire on unarmed Bostonians and kill five; the colonists use the term "Boston Massacre" to stir up anti-British sentiment.

**1773**
Parliament passes the Tea Act.

**1773**
Disguised as Mohawk Indians, colonists dump British tea into Boston Harbor at the "Boston Tea Party."

**1774**
Parliament passes several measures to clamp down on the colonies. The colonists label the legislation the "Intolerable Acts."

**April 1775**
The Revolutionary War begins at Lexington and Concord.

**May 1775**
The Second Continental Congress convenes in Philadelphia; Massachusetts sends five delegates.

**June 1775**
George Washington is nominated by John Adams and elected commander in chief of the newly formed Continental army.

**June 1775**
The Battle of Bunker Hill is fought on Breed's Hill in Charlestown, near Boston. Americans inflict heavy casualties on British troops before ceding the territory.

**March 1776**
The British are forced out of Boston, marking a turning point in the war. The Continental army forces the British out of Boston.

**July 1776**
The Declaration of Independence is adopted at the Second Continental Congress; John Adams serves on the five-person committee charged with drafting the declaration.

**1780**
The Massachusetts Constitution, written by John Adams, goes into effect.

**1781**
The Articles of Confederation go into effect.

**October 1781**
The British army, under General Charles Cornwallis, surrenders at Yorktown, Virginia. This is the last major battle of the Revolutionary War.

**September 1783**
Great Britain signs the Treaty of Paris, officially ending the Revolutionary War and ceding its land to the Americans.

**1786–1787**
Daniel Shays leads an uprising of hundreds of men in western Massachusetts. Shays's Rebellion raises concerns that government under the Articles of Confederation is too weak.

**May 1787**
The Constitutional Convention opens in Philadelphia. Massachusetts sends delegates Elbridge Gerry, Nathaniel Gorham, Rufus King, and Caleb Strong.

**February 1788**
Massachusetts becomes the sixth state to ratify the U.S. Constitution.

# For Further Reading

Clifford Lindsey Alderman, *The Story of the Thirteen Colonies*. New York: Random House, 1966. This historical account of each of the colonies includes a chapter, "Pilgrims and Puritans," that tells of the first settlements of Massachusetts.

Daniel J. Boorstin, *The Landmark History of the American People: From Plymouth to Appomattox*. New York: Random House, 1987. A book written for everybody, covering the major events of the colonial period and early American history.

Christopher Collier and James Lincoln Collier, *Pilgrims and Puritans*. New York: Benchmark Books, 1998. Recounts the religious, political, and social history of the Massachusetts Bay Colony and its influence on our lives today.

James Daugherty, *The Landing of the Pilgrims*. New York: Landmark Books, 1978. The story of the Plymouth settlers, from their life in England, to their settlement in Holland, to their voyage on the *Mayflower*, to their first years in the New World.

Karen Doherty, *William Bradford: Rock of Plymouth*. Brookfield, CT: Twenty-first Century Books, 1999. A biography of the Pilgrim leader who would serve as the second governor of Plymouth Plantation. This book gives particular attention to his role in establishing and maintaining the settlement. The book relies heavily on, and quotes from, Bradford's book *Of Plimouth Plantation*.

Frank Dwyer, *John Adams*. New York: Chelsea House, 1989. A biography of this Massachusetts leader, with an introduction entitled "On Leadership" by Arthur M. Schlesinger Jr.

Howard Egger-Bovet and Marlene Smith-Baranzini, *Book of the American Colonies*. Boston: Little, Brown, 1996. Discusses the reasons Europeans settled in America, the growth of the original colonies, daily life in colonial America, and the reaction to the newcomers of the people already living in the New World. Includes firsthand accounts, diary entries, letters, speeches, and activities.

Dennis B. Fradin, *The Massachusetts Colony*. Chicago: Childrens Press, 1987. The story of colonial Massachusetts, from the Native Americans who settled the land to the first explorers and the American Revolution. Includes biographical sketches of notable people of colonial Massachusetts and important Massachusetts documents.

———, *Samuel Adams: The Father of American Independence*. New York: Clarion Books, 1998. This biography of Samuel Adams offers a detailed look at the events that took place in Massachusetts leading up to, during, and following the American Revolution.

Joy Hakim, *Making Thirteen Colonies*. New York: Oxford University Press, 1993. A lively narrative of life in the New World, with a lot of interesting details about the New England Puritans. Sidebars, maps, vintage documents, and other illustrations help bring history to life for young people.

Suzanne LeVert, *Celebrate the States: Massachusetts*. New York: Benchmark Books, 2000. A beautifully illustrated book that tells of Massachusetts today and how its history has affected the people and culture.

Cyril Leek Marshall, *The Mayflower Destiny*. Harrisburg, PA: Stackpole Books, 1975. Written in conjunction with Plymouth Plantation, this illustrated book tells how the settlers of Plymouth lived.

Sylvia McNair, Massachusetts. Danbury, CT: Childrens Press, 1998. Part of the America the Beautiful series, this book provides information about the land and people of Massachusetts.

# Works Consulted

**Books**

Douglass Adair and John A. Schutz, eds., *Peter Oliver's Origin and Progress of the American Rebellion: A Tory View.* Stanford, CA: Stanford University Press, 1967. A historical account of the American Revolution written in 1781 by Peter Oliver, a British loyalist living in Massachusetts during the time.

Catherine Drinker Bowen, *Miracle at Philadelphia.* Boston: Little, Brown, 1986. A highly readable and detailed account of the Constitutional Convention, beginning with the arrival of the delegates in Philadelphia and ending with the ratification of the Constitution.

William Bradford, *Of Plimouth Plantation.* New York: Paragon Books, 1962. A firsthand account that describes the Pilgrims' experience as they crossed the Atlantic Ocean and settled in Plymouth, Massachusetts.

Hugh Brogan, *The Penguin History of the United States of America.* New York: Penguin Books, 1990. A comprehensive history of the United States, written for general audiences.

Richard D. Brown, *Massachusetts.* New York: W. W. Norton, 1978. Published in cooperation with the American Association for State and Local History, a historical account of Massachusetts, from the difficulties faced by the early colonists at Plymouth and Massachusetts Bay to the challenges faced by twentieth-century residents as a result of ever-increasing ethnic and cultural diversity.

James MacGregor Burns, J. W. Peltason, Thomas E. Cronin, and David B. Magleby, *Government by the People.* 16th ed. Englewood Cliffs, NJ: Prentice-Hall, 1995. A textbook account of U.S. government.

David Brion Davis and Steven Mintz, *The Boisterous Sea of Liberty.* New York: Oxford University Press, 1998. A documentary history of America from discovery through the Civil War.

Frank M. Fahey and Marie L. Fahey, *Chapters from the American Experience: Volume One.* Englewood Cliffs, NJ: Prentice-Hall, 1971. Description of events in early American history, from the colonial days to the mid-1800s. The book includes many firsthand accounts of those who were there.

Robert G. Ferris and James H. Charleton, *The Signers of the Constitution.* Flagstaff, AZ: Interpretive Publications, 1986. This book provides a straightforward account of the historical events that took place in Philadelphia in 1787 and short biographical sketches of each of the men who signed the resulting Constitution.

Oscar and Lilian Handlin, *Liberty and Power: 1600–1760.* New York: Harper & Row, 1986. The first of four volumes; an account of America's colonial history.

Richard Hofstadter, *America at 1750: A Social Portrait.* New York: Random House, 1973. A description of the colonial population in the mid–eighteenth century.

Benjamin W. Labaree, *Colonial Massachusetts: A History.* Millwood, NY: KTO Press, 1979. A lively and comprehensive history of colonial Massachusetts, from the settlement of the Pilgrims and Puritans to the drafting of the new state constitution.

Douglas Edward Leach, *The Northern Colonial Frontier: 1607–1763.* New York: Holt, Rinehart & Winston, 1966. A history of the white settlement of the northeastern United States, focusing particular attention on the early pioneers' quest for land and the conflicts that resulted among European nations and with the indigenous peoples of the region.

Kenneth A. Lockridge, *A New England Town: The First Hundred Years.* New York: W. W. Norton, 1970. The story of the town of Dedham, Massachusetts, and the changes it went through from its founding in 1636 until the middle of the eighteenth century.

Milton Lomask, *The Spirit of 1787: The Making of the Constitution.* New York: Farrar Straus & Giroux, 1980. An easy-to-read account of the Constitutional Convention, beginning with the "Critical

Period" under the Articles of Confederation and ending with ratification of the Constitution.

Bonnie L. Lukes, *The Boston Massacre*. San Diego: Lucent Books, 1998. An interesting and lively account of the events leading up to and following March 5, 1770, the day that British soldiers fired on unarmed civilians in Boston.

Jill Maynard, ed., *Through Indian Eyes: The Untold Story of Native American Peoples*. Pleasantville, NY: Reader's Digest, 1995. The history of America as experienced by Native Americans, amplified by illustrations and memorable quotations from native people, past and present.

Philip McFarland, *The Brave Bostonians: Hutchinson, Quincy, Franklin, and the Coming of the American Revolution*. Boulder, CO: Westview Press, 1998. The story of the events that took place in Boston leading up to the American Revolution, focusing on the Bostonians who influenced these events.

Richard Middleton, *Colonial America: A History, 1585–1776*. Cambridge, MA: Blackwell, 1996. A historical account of colonial America, from the exploration of the New World to the American Revolution.

———, *Colonial America: A History, 1607–1760*. Cambridge, MA: Blackwell, 1992. A historical account of colonial America, from the beginning of the first colony at Jamestown to the events leading up to the American Revolution.

Edmund S. Morgan, *The Birth of the Republic: 1763–89*. Chicago: University of Chicago Press, 1977. A short history of the events that transformed the thirteen colonies into a nation, beginning with the events leading up to the American Revolution and ending with the ratification of the Constitution.

Samuel Eliot Morison, *The Maritime History of Massachusetts: 1783–1860*. Boston: Houghton Mifflin, 1941. A detailed and dense history of the maritime enterprise of Massachusetts—shipping, seaborne commerce, whaling, and fishing—and the influence the state's close ties with the sea had on the history of Massachusetts and the United States.

Sumner Chilton Powell, *Puritan Village: The Formation of a New England Town.* Hanover, NH: Wesleyan University Press, 1963. A Pulitzer Prize–winning account of the early government and social organization of the town of Sudbury, Massachusetts.

Jerome R. Reich, *Colonial America,* 4th ed. Upper Saddle River, NJ: Prentice-Hall, 1998. An easy-to-read and easy-to-follow description of life in colonial America.

Alan Simpson, *Puritanism in Old and New England.* Chicago: University of Chicago Press, 1972. This series of six essays sketches the impact of Puritanism on English and American institutions in the seventeenth century and beyond.

Page Smith, *A New Age Now Begins.* New York: McGraw-Hill, 1976. A detailed narrative of the birth of the United States of America in three volumes.

Felix Sutton, *Sons of Liberty.* New York: Julian Messner, 1969. Focusing on the people who were instrumental in colonial resistance to English rule, the book's heroes are almost all from Massachusetts. Chapters focus on Massachusetts statesmen Samuel Adams, John Hancock, Paul Revere, and Joseph Warren.

Dale Taylor, *A Writer's Guide to Everyday Life in Colonial America.* Cincinnati, OH: Writer's Digest Books, 1987. A fact-filled book with descriptions of life in the colonies, including details about everyday life, government, trade, and colonial society.

Francis Newton Thorpe, *The Federal and State Constitutions, Colonial Charters, and Other Organic Laws of the States, Territories, and Colonies Now or Heretofore Forming the United States of America.* Washington, DC: Government Printing Office, 1909. A collection of documents used to govern the colonies, territories, and states prior to the twentieth century.

Alexis de Tocqueville, *Democracy in America.* New York: New American Library, 1956. A firsthand account of American life, written by a French visitor.

Edwin Tunis, *Colonial Living.* New York: Thomas Y. Crowell, 1957. A re-creation of seventeenth- and eighteenth-century America that brings to life the everyday lives of the men and women who transplanted and adapted European culture to the New World.

Clarence L. Ver Steeg and Richard Hofstadter, *Great Issues in American History: From Settlement to Revolution, 1584–1776.* Vol. 1. New York: Vintage Books, 1969. Primary sources related to the history of colonial America.

**Internet Sources**

Department of Humanities Computing, University of Groningen, "Resolutions of the Stamp Act Congress." Text prepared for "The American Revolution: An HTML Project," 1997. www.let.rug.nl/~usa/D/1751-1775/stampact/sa.htm.

President and Fellows of Harvard College, "The Harvard Guide: An Introduction," 2001. www.hno.harvard.edu/guide/intro.

John Winthrop, "A Modell of Christian Charity," written for the Massachusetts Bay Colony, 1630, as quoted on www.libertynet. org/~edcivic/winthrop.html.

**Websites**

**Department of Humanities Computing,** University of Groningen, "The American Revolution: An HTML Project, 1997. (www.let. rug.nl/~usa). This website includes original documents from the period leading up to and during the Revolutionary War, essays written about the documents and events, and links to a host of other Internet resources.

**Massachusetts Historical Society** (www.masshist.org). This site provides a wealth of information and links regarding the history of Massachusetts.

# Index

# Picture Credits

Dover Publications, 51, 60

Hulton Getty Collection/Archive Photos, 19, 67

Library of Congress, 9, 29, 58, 59, 71

National Archives, 74

North Wind Picture Archives, 11, 13, 15, 16, 22, 23, 26, 30, 36, 37, 40, 42, 44, 46, 52, 54, 69

Stock Montage, Inc., 32

Stock Montage, Inc./The Newberry Library, 41

# About the Author

Lydia Bjornlund is a private consultant and freelance writer, focusing primarily on issues related to civic education, government, and training. She is the author of more than a dozen books and training manuals. This is her fourth book for Lucent Books.

Ms. Bjornlund holds a master of education degree from Harvard University and a bachelor of arts from Williams College, where she majored in American studies. She lives in Oakton, Virginia, with her husband, Gerry Hoetmer, and their children, Jake and Sophia.